# LIGHTS! CAMERA! ARKANSAS!

# LIGHTS!
# CAMERA!
# ARKANSAS!

## From Broncho Billy to Billy Bob Thornton

### ROBERT COCHRAN
### SUZANNE McCRAY

The University of Arkansas Press

Fayetteville

2015

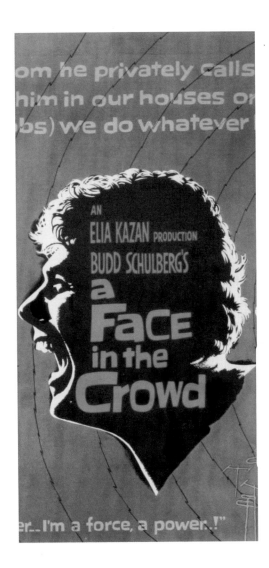

Copyright © 2015 by The University of Arkansas Press

Printed in Canada

ISBN: 978-1-55728-672-7
e-ISBN-13: 978-1-61075-558-0

19  18  17  16  15     5  4  3  2  1

*Designed by Liz Lester*

LIBRARY OF CONGRESS CONTROL NUMBER:
2014919538

This project was funded in part by the Old State House Museum.

Acrylic Paintings: x, 19, 21, 23, 26, 28, 30, 38, 40, 58, 59, 62, 70 and 76. © 2012 Patterson and Barnes. Images from the Old State House Museum Collection.

# Contents

IN 1946 THIS MAN KILLED FIVE PEOPLE...
TODAY HE STILL LURKS THE STREETS OF TEXARKANA, ARK.

*Charles B. Pierce's* "THE TOWN THAT DREADED SUNDOWN"

A TRUE STORY

Starring
**BEN JOHNSON** · ANDREW PRINE · DAWN WELLS as Helen Reed
Written by EARL E. SMITH · Produced and Directed by CHARLES B. PIERCE
An AMERICAN INTERNATIONAL RELEASE

**R** RESTRICTED

7275

"THE TOWN THAT DREADED SUNDOWN"

# Introduction

This volume is written to accompany *Lights! Camera! Arkansas!,* an exhibit mounted by the Old State House Museum in Little Rock from 2013 to 2015, but it aspires as well to serve as a first attempt at a general survey of Arkansas and Arkansans in Hollywood films. The general model is identical to that deployed in 1996 and 2003, with the two *Our Own Sweet Sounds* exhibits devoted to Arkansas music. That catalog, after two editions, was followed by the more comprehensively inclusive *Encyclopedia of Arkansas Music.* The assumption is straightforward—a first attempt, if executed with sufficient competency to at least suggest the project's plausibility, will eventually lead to greater attention to these films and the artists who made them.

We owe thanks first to Bill Gatewood and Jo Ellen Maack, who invited Robert Cochran to serve as guest curator for *Lights! Camera! Arkansas!* and encouraged the two of us to work together on the accompanying catalog. For our part, we regarded the opportunity as heaven sent—for many years, as we worked on one after another of our separate projects, we had hoped for a chance to do a book together as coauthors.

What could be better, we thought, than sitting at home watching films, eating popcorn, and writing up what we learned? Through most of 2013 we kept at it steadily, sometimes with guests but most often just the two of us, enjoying triumphs like *A Face in the Crowd, The Accountant,* and *Two-Lane Blacktop* and rolling our eyes at losers like *The Monster and the Stripper, So Sad about Gloria,* and *Chopper Chicks in Zombietown.* Before we finished, we'd taken in some two hundred pictures—our best and worst nominees are highlighted in the appendix "Picks and Pans."

Many people helped us along the way. We first learned of Freeman Owens (and William Lighton and Marty Stouffer) from Frank Scheide. Ellen Compton told us about the apparently lost *Wonder Valley,* filmed on location in Cave Springs in the 1950s. Dale Carpenter loaned us his own video portrait of "Broncho Billy" Anderson and led us to the pioneering documentary work of Jack Hill. Our direct citations of Phillip

Martin barely hint at his guidance—whole evenings have been given to cruising his *blood, dirt & angels* blog. Larry Foley was especially helpful with information about the Hot Springs Documentary Film Festival and the pioneering documentary work at AETN. At the Niles Essanay Silent Film Museum in Fremont, California, David Kiehn treated us to a special behind-the-scenes tour. Back in 2007, Derek Jenkins, serving as guest editor of the *Oxford American*'s "Southern Movie Issue," shared films by Phil Chambliss. Yancey Prosser helped on several occasions, most memorably by making available Daniel Campbell's award-winning shorts. Peggy Lloyd alerted us just as we finished to the busy Hollywood career of Trevor Bardette.

Thanks are also due to the University of Arkansas Press for turning our manuscript into an attractive book and to our supervisors at the University of Arkansas who supported and encouraged this work at the margins of our usual fields of endeavor. We're especially grateful to Mike Bieker, Brian King, Melissa King, and Tyler Lail from the former group, and from the latter Suzanne McCray thanks especially Chancellor G. David Gearhart, Provost Sharon Gaber, Dean Tom Smith of the College of Education and Health Professions, and Ketevan Mamiseishvili, department chair of rehabilitation, human resources, and communication disorders, while Robert Cochran is most grateful to Fulbright College Dean Todd Shields, Associate Dean Lynda Coon, and English Department Chair Dorothy Stephens.

Finally, ending where we started, this has been an Old State House Museum project from beginning to end—as we worked, we visited the exhibit repeatedly, notepads in hand, listening to the wonderful interviews with Jeff Nichols, Mary Steenburgen, and Joey Lauren Adams in the video; jotting down names from the wall of photographs in the entrance foyer; and wandering again and again past Gail Moore Stephens's beautifully arranged exhibit cases and the striking paintings produced by Gary Patterson and Marion Barnes. We rushed out to purchase Hal Needham's memoir, *Stuntman!,* at Jo Ellen Maack's recommendation, and Bill Gatewood, at the very beginning, wisely urged us to give *The Accountant* our closest attention.

This is a richly illustrated volume thanks to the work of Jo Ellen Maack, who selected every image. Our year of watching, scribbling, and discussing was a rollicking pleasure, and our goals for this first survey of Arkansas's ongoing engagement with film will be realized if it serves as a worthy companion to the work of Bill, Gail, Jo Ellen, and their colleagues at the Old State House Museum. Thanks to all.

ROBERT COCHRAN, SUZANNE McCRAY
*April 20, 2014*

BRONCHO BILLY

# Hollywood, Arkansas

## *"Broncho Billy," Uncle Tom, and Hallelujah*

Hollywood, Arkansas—doesn't sound quite right, does it (though a town of that name once existed in Clark County)? On the one hand, Tinsel Town seems glamorous and ephemeral, a purveyor of the nation's dreams with its red carpet ablaze in neon and flashbulbs. On the other, Arkansas leads with Ozark cabins, Delta plantations, shadowed swamplands, deer stands and duck blinds with sturdy forebears blazing away. Unlikely partners it might seem, a town founded upon fantasy and a region knee-deep in tradition.

But as it turns out, stereotypes aside, Arkansas and Hollywood have been dancing together nicely since the first cameras rolled. The whole range is on view, from best to worst, timeless classics to god-awful turkeys. Arkansans on both sides of the camera have contributed to everything from musicals to oaters. They have played Huck Finn innocents and homicidal sociopaths, noir detectives and cowboy gunslingers, bathing beauties menaced by prehistoric creatures. The story of the Natural State's role in the nation's film entertainment mecca is a tangled, compelling tale full of surprises. Recent years have been spectacularly fruitful, but the roots run deep. Arkansas has been from territorial times a place of mythic resonance (Twain and Melville knew it), and Hollywood was sure to come calling.

Act one opens with two men from Pine Bluff and Little Rock who at one point crossed paths in Chicago. One was a technical wizard whose name never appeared in lights, and the other became Hollywood's first

Gilbert "Broncho Billy" Anderson.

cowboy star. The older of the two, the future cowpuncher Gilbert Maxwell Aronson (1880–1971), was born in Little Rock and worked briefly in St. Louis and in his brother-in-law's cotton brokerage in Pine Bluff in the 1890s. Around 1900 he headed for New York, where he changed his name to Gilbert Anderson, took up acting, and in 1903 used a bald-faced lie (reportedly claiming the horsemanship skills of a Texas Ranger) to get hired for Edwin S. Porter's pioneering western, *The Great Train Robbery*. Though his lack of even basic riding skills was soon apparent—he was apparently tossed at least twice, the first time at the stable when he tried to climb on from the wrong side—Anderson made it into the film in several unmounted roles, coming on as a bandit, getting shot as a passenger attempting to escape, and dancing to gunfire as a tenderfoot in a dance-hall scene.

Sensing opportunity's arrival in what was then a novel entertainment technology, Anderson jumped in with both feet. By 1905 he'd added directing to his résumé with *Raffles, the Amateur Cracksman*, the first film treatment of E. W. Hornung's popular "gentleman thief" stories (John Barrymore starred in a longer version in 1917). The next year Anderson moved west to Chicago to work for William N. Selig's Polyscope Company. Selig and Anderson ended up not getting along, but three 1907 productions (*The Girl from Montana*, *The Bandit King*, and *Western Justice*) were the novice director's first experience with on-location work in western films.

The bigger move came when Anderson established Essanay Studios in partnership with George K. Spoor (Spoor and Anderson, S&A, "Essanay") and began turning out films at a furious rate, launching a series of westerns with *Broncho Billy's Redemption* in 1910. Anderson was an unlikely cowboy star, a beefy gent who still had a lot to learn about horses, but he worked steadily, churning out "good bad guy" melodramas. By 1912, relocated to the more suitable landscapes (and weather) of California, Essanay could crank out a "Broncho Billy" two-reeler in a week. The following year alone Anderson made more than thirty pictures, starting with *Broncho Billy and the Maid* in January and calling it a year with *Broncho Billy's Christmas Deed* in December. Costing less than $1,000 each, some grossed as much as $50,000.

Plots were straightforwardly formulaic, with lots of riding and shooting and sentimental pieties invariably triumphant. The loner western hero, a man stripped of home and family, accompanied by no woman, and always galloping out of town as the curtain falls, was a later development. If Broncho Billy, at the headwaters of the tradition, comes in as a vagabond outlaw, a figure of the shadowy margin, the narrative typically carries him by the end toward society's centers. Anderson and Spoor marketed their films as family entertainment and moral uplift. The favored agents of redemption are children, but women and clergymen often fill in. The Bible is a frequent prop. *Broncho Billy and the School Mistress* (1912) closes (after Billy survives a shooting by his romantic rival) upon rejoicing children cheering beside a sign reading "School Closed: Teacher Married Broncho Billy." The appallingly stereotyped *Bronco Billy and the Greaser* (1913) features Anderson rescuing a young female homesteader menaced by a vaguely nonwhite villain (he's labeled "Half Breed" in the cast list) and then being rescued in turn by a posse summoned by the grateful woman. Bible lessons from a kindly preacher's wife redeem Billy from a life of crime in *Broncho Billy's Sentence* (1915)—he's eventually pardoned after a stint as a jailhouse evangelist.

These pieties proved immensely popular—before Anderson was done, he'd turned out nearly 150 Broncho Billy titles (among a total output of close to 500 films) and in the process made himself into a wealthy and widely recognized figure, the new industry's first cowboy star. By 1918 Broncho Billy was done—his last ride was *The Son-of-a-Gun*, though Anderson went on to earn a secondary niche in film annals by producing Stan Laurel's first pairing with Oliver Hardy (*The Lucky Dog*, released in 1921). Twenty-five years of obscurity followed, but Anderson lived long enough to receive an honorary Oscar in 1957 for his pioneering contributions. There was also a final cameo in 1965 when he appeared with other old-time western stars in *The Bounty Killer*.

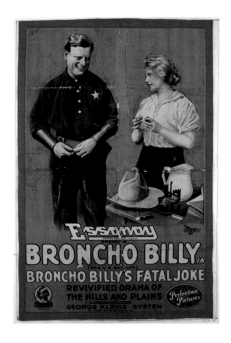

Gilbert M. Anderson
with Oscar, 1957.

Freeman Owens at Work.

Arkansas's other pioneer, Pine Bluff native Freeman Harrison Owens (1890–1979), was a decade younger than Anderson. A self-taught mechanical genius, he was drawn to cinema early. At twelve he was sweeping up and turning the hand-cranked projector at the local theater, and by 1908 he'd dropped out of high school, designed his own camera, and was adding local footage to screenings. Soon he was shooting all over the country for the first generation of newsreels—he filmed the Chicago Stock Yard fire of 1910 and the Charleston (South Carolina) hurricane and flood of 1911. In 1912 he signed with Anderson at Essanay, where he worked with the era's biggest stars (Wallace Beery, Charlie Chaplin, Douglas Fairbanks, and Gloria Swanson).

Owens spent World War I in the Marine Corps Reserves as a cameraman, shooting propaganda films (*Flying with the Marines*, 1918) and pioneering the techniques of aerial photography. At least one source lists him as an "ace" pilot in addition to his camera skills. Back home after the Armistice, he resumed his news work, filming horseraces (Man O' War) and prizefights (Jack Dempsey) and using his new slow-motion camera to capture Babe Ruth's home-run swing in 1920.

Even more significant than these varied adventures were Owens's many inventions crucial to the growth of the film industry—slow-motion cameras, synchronized sound, early 3-D technology, wide-angle lenses, home-movie projectors, plastic lenses, and the A. C. Nielsen rating system for measuring the audiences of radio and television shows. All in all, he was awarded some two hundred patents. Owens retired to Pine Bluff in the early 1970s.

The writer William Rheem Lighton (1866–1923) was born in Pennsylvania but became best known for his 1914 celebration of his Fayetteville home, *Happy Hollow Farm*. He wrote the screenplay for the western comedy *Water, Water Everywhere* (1920), with Will Rogers in the lead role. It was his only film, though Lighton's son, Louis (1895–1963), forged a durable screenwriting and producing career—he shared writing credits with his wife, Hope Loring, for *Wings* (1927), winner of the initial Oscar for Best Picture in 1929 (it was called Outstanding Picture then), and several films he produced were Oscar winners as well. Spencer Tracy picked up the Oscar for Best Actor in 1937 for *Captains Courageous,* and James Dunn won as Best Supporting Actor in *A Tree Grows in Brooklyn* in 1945.

Arkansas first appeared as a location for Hollywood films in 1926, when Universal Pictures came to Helena to shoot riverboat scenes for *Uncle Tom's Cabin* aboard the sternwheeler *Kate Adams.* The film itself, shot mostly in Mississippi and Louisiana, was a huge undertaking—studio publicity repeatedly stressed its nearly $2,000,000 price tag. Director Harry A. Pollard spent $20,000 on purebred bloodhounds and rechanneled the Los Angeles River for Eliza's climactic escape across the ice. The Arkansas segment didn't come cheap, either, since weekly rent on the *Kate Adams* (which also required extensive renovation) reportedly ran to $4,350.

The result of all this expenditure was a bizarre film, a muddled mix of liberal-for-the-day and retrograde "old plantation" elements wrapped up in Hollywood's very latest in lavish production, including cutting-edge special effects allowing for Little Eva's ascent to heaven and Uncle Tom's posthumous return as a vengeful ghost. Responsibility for the strange mix seems to lie squarely with Pollard. A proud southerner, he traced his family to Kentucky and Virginia, assuring worried studio executives at the outset that he would produce no film offensive to Dixie. His version of Harriet Beecher Stowe's perennial story, seventy years after its initial publication, would somehow celebrate both abolitionist triumphs and the plantation South.

An impossible undertaking, clearly, but Pollard gave it his all. The opening tableau features Robert E. Lee joining Stowe's abolitionist team with his pre–Civil War description of slavery as a "moral and political evil," even as the film's original opening slave-market scene was cut from the final version in an attempt to appease southern opposition—the Memphis chapter of the United Daughters of the Confederacy went public with its disapproval of the whole project. Another bow to the Daughters follows shortly, as the benign but hapless Shelbys are introduced with a title card proclaiming their "gentle rule of the slaves" as "typical of the South." But then Abraham Lincoln also gets a cameo, proclaiming emancipation of the slaves, and Union troops (Pollard

*Uncle Tom's Cabin* (1927).

having moved Stowe's storyline forward to include the war the novel only foreshadowed) are shown tromping through the Southland, Old Glory waving triumphantly. The Daughters were surely horrified by such scenes, but Pollard provides another sop—Simon Legree, the tale's arch villain, is introduced by a title card specifying his nonsouthern origins. He "came from the North," viewers are assured, and "bore an evil reputation for cruelty to his slaves."

James B. Lowe was not the first African American actor to play Uncle Tom. That was Sam Lucas (in a 1914 version), but Lowe's portrayal became the iconic film image. Universal even sent him to England to promote the film, making Lowe, in cinema historian Donald Bogle's estimation, the first black actor to be celebrated in studio publicity. But Tom, for all his strength and forbearance, is largely moved to the background in Pollard's treatment. He's on screen for fewer than ten minutes of the nearly two-hour film, though another radical revision of Stowe's novel allows his ghostly return to beckon the villainous Legree to his death.

Pollard also shifts primary focus to female characters. Feminist critics, Michele Wallace preeminent among them, have noted that enslaved women act effectively to free themselves from bondage and that in particular Topsy, often viewed as a crude caricature, is presented in more complex terms, especially in her loving relationship with Little Eva. In short, despite the film's repeated lapses into demeaning stereotype, not only are Stowe's abolitionist themes clearly highlighted, but slaves themselves also are portrayed as active agents in pursuit of their freedom. The United Daughters of the Confederacy, clinging to their happy plantation fantasies, had good reason for their misgivings, and Arkansas made its Hollywood debut in a film that's still powerful after almost ninety years, at once uplifting and disturbing, thrilling and embarrassing.

Just two years after the 1927 release of *Uncle Tom's Cabin*, eastern Arkansas landscapes made a second Hollywood appearance when director King Vidor, flush from the success of *The Big Parade* (1925) and his Oscar nomination for *The Crowd* in 1928, chose several Crittenden County locations for his sound-film debut. *Hallelujah*, released in 1929, a big-budget musical starring an entirely African American cast, is arguably the most historically significant film with Arkansas ties. Vidor wanted to make it so badly he persuaded reluctant studio bosses by putting his own money behind it.

If Vidor's vision in *Hallelujah* was to create a film presenting blacks straightforwardly without stereotype, he had his work cut out for him. Critic Thomas Cripps points out that 80 percent of 1920s film roles for African Americans were as maids or butlers. Lee Daniels' recent film *The Butler* (2013) perfectly captures the role of the black servant—the room is to appear empty if he is the only one in it. Africans Americans and children were to be seen and not heard. Vidor works to remove this cloak of invisibility and record the vibrant voice of African American life.

Vidor was clearly not afraid of a challenge. Deciding to escape Hollywood, he filmed in Arkansas and Tennessee, hoping to escape the stereotyped vision of the always-happy, not-too-bright devoted servant whose only goal is to make life a little easier for the white employer. Like *Uncle Tom's Cabin, Hallelujah* goes a long way to undermine this view, though unlike *Uncle Tom's Cabin,* none of *Hallelujah*'s actors are whites in blackface.

Did Vidor completely escape stereotyping blacks? The answer is clearly no. When in 2006 Warner Home Video released the film in conjunction with Turner Broadcasting, the packaging included a detailed disclaimer, reading in part: "The films you are about to see are a product of their time." There is good reason for this—Vidor's film, while pushing boundaries for its time, often comes across as offensively racist to contemporary viewers.

The film pulses with Vidor's understanding of African American sexuality and religious ecstasy, often blending the two. A much quoted except from Vidor's autobiography, *A Tree Is a Tree,* emphasizes his desire to make "a film about Negroes, using only Negroes in the cast. The sincerity and fervor of their religious expression intrigued me, as did the honest simplicity of their sexual drives. In many instances the intermingling of these two activities seems to offer striking dramatic content." In the film the battle between the physical and the spiritual drive the narrative.

Before the first scene opens, we hear an insistent drumbeat, then shift to a series of brief excerpts from spirituals ("Hallelujah," "Let My People Go," and "Motherless Child") as the screen displays a cotton field in Wilson, Arkansas—a town named for Robert E. Lee Wilson, the largest employer in the area at that time.

Daniel L. Haynes, a college-educated African American, plays Zeke Johnson, a sharecropper who is entrusted by his family with the year's cotton crop. He is expected to sell it, which he does, and to return with his younger brother Spunk, who accompanies him, and their earnings, which he does not. Zeke is tempted instead by drink, gambling, and the lovely Chick (played by the teenage, then-unknown Nina Mae McKinney), who along with her lover tricks him out of the family's money. When Zeke understands that he has been tricked, he becomes violent, waving a gun and shooting randomly into the room, fatally wounding Spunk.

His family forgives Zeke, whose conversations with his preacher-father lead to a none-too-subtle salvation experience, with light coming out of the darkness to make visible the legitimacy of his conversion. A placard announces "And Zekiel Became a Preacher." And preach he does, riding among his flock on a donkey like the Messiah himself triumphantly entering Jerusalem.

The film focuses on this fight between good and evil. Farm life, hard work, family, a good woman, and religion, these are clearly the saving choices. But the lights of town, the lure of gambling, and a faithless woman pull him in a different direction. Choosing between Sunday morning and Saturday night proves too much for Zeke, especially when the two are overtly brought together at the

*Hallelujah* (1929).

church meeting immediately following his marriage proposal to Missy Rose (played by blues singer Victoria Spivey). Chick attends and seems to be moved by the spirit, but she is clearly attempting once again to capture Zeke's attention, making her intentions clear when she bites his hand. He understands the message and carries her off, headed back to the city and to work in the timber mills.

Removed from family, from the land he knows how to work, from church, and from his rightful bride, Zeke is clearly trouble bound. Chick soon tires of working-class life and runs off with her former lover, Hot Shot (William Fountain). Zeke pursues them, with Chick dying accidentally in the ensuing chase, apologizing for her ways with her final breath while cradled in Zeke's arms. He then chases down and murders Hot

Shot in the nearby swamp. The killing of Spunk had been accidental, but Hot Shot's death is a deliberate, brutal execution.

Zeke has now hit bottom, sunk as low as he can go. But hard labor in prison reforms him, and he returns at last to his family, his land, and his good woman. All will now be well. Vidor's film moves from the stereotypic ever-happy African American to the truly happy man. Zeke strikes a contemporary viewer as anything but a quick study, yet he does learn from his experiences. In Vidor's film the ultimate goal is not to make an employer happy (employers—and whites generally as Ryan Friedman points out in *Hollywood's African American Films*—are strikingly absent from the film), but for Zeke to find happiness and a right livelihood for himself. This is a significant step forward for the time and may help explain why many critics today still commend Vidor's and *Hallelujah*'s ambitions and achievements even as they point out the lapses.

After *Hallelujah,* a decade passed before an Arkansas scene next appeared on the big screen. *Gone with the Wind* was a blockbuster, a film as big as films got, but to describe Arkansas's role as a cameo would greatly overstate the case. Reach for the popcorn and you could miss it, a glimpse in the opening credits of North Little Rock's Old Mill, built in 1933 to look like a nineteenth-century water-powered gristmill. It's there today, described for visitors as the last *Gone with the Wind* structure still standing. The film itself, however, does feature a more substantial connection to Arkansas in the character of the house servant Pork, played by Marianna native Oscar Polk (1899–1949). Polk was already an established Broadway actor, with roles in *The Green Pastures* (1935) and *You Can't Take It with You* (1936), among others. He'd also appeared in films, including famed African American director Oscar Micheaux's *Underworld* in 1937. (He would also be in the same director's *The Notorious Elinor Lee* in 1940 following his appearance in *Gone with the Wind*.) Polk died in New York City, run down by a cab when he stepped from a curb in Times Square.

Oscar Polk.

As Hollywood's film industry took hold and flourished, other Arkansans heard the movies' siren song and headed for California in pursuit of fame and fortune. Robin Burn (1890–1956), probably born in Greenwood and certainly raised in Van Buren, first gained notice as musical comic and cornpone "Arkansas Philosopher" Bob Burns on the radio, but in the 1930s and 1940s, he also made films, inaugurating a durable tradition of Arkansas musicians padding their résumés with Hollywood work. In his first star turns—*Rhythm on the Range* (1936) and *Waikiki Wedding* (1937)—he's paired with Bing Crosby. The 1930s also saw the first Weaver Brothers and Elviry films, spinoffs of the Arkansas Travelers, a popular musical-comedy act pioneered by Missouri brothers Leon and Frank Weaver. Elviry was June Weaver, married first to Leon and later to Frank, with no rupture of their professional collaboration. Two films, *Down in 'Arkansaw'* (1938) and *Arkansas Judge* (1941), set in Pine Ridge and Peaceful Valley, Arkansas, respectively, mix positive traits of generosity, hospitality, and native intelligence with the standard hillbilly stereotypes. Roy Rogers makes a rare appearance in the latter movie as a noncowboy (he's a lawyer).

Many Arkansas women also found success during Hollywood's early years. The state's first film actress may have been Little Rock's Barbara Castleton (1894–1978), who from 1914 to 1923 appeared in more than twenty-five silent films, including the 1917 picture *For the Freedom of the World*. She plays a new bride who disguises herself as a nurse in order to accompany her ace-pilot husband to France. The state's other pioneer actresses include Katharine Alexander, Peggy Shannon, sisters Evelyn and Betty Francisco, Janet Chandler, Irene Castle, and Ann Gillis.

Barbara Castleton.

Katharine Alexander.

Alexander (1898–1977), born in Fort Smith, was on stage in New York before she turned twenty and by 1924 had risen to starring roles, playing the title character in *That Awful Mrs. Eaton*. By the mid-1930s she was working steadily in Hollywood, appearing in supporting roles in more than forty films, including *The Painted Veil* (1934, with Greta Garbo), *That Certain Woman* (1937, with Bette Davis), and *In Name Only* (1939, with Cary Grant). Her greatest triumph came late, with her 1949 London stage performance as Linda Loman in *Death of a Salesman*. In retirement Alexander returned to Fort Smith, where she apparently lived happily until her death.

Peggy Shannon (1907–1941) had no such luck. Almost a decade younger than Alexander, Shannon was born Winona Sammon in Pine Bluff and first got noticed on a 1923 trip with her mother to visit an aunt in New York. The aunt, it turned out, shared an apartment building with Florenz Ziegfeld's secretary, who knew a beauty when she saw one. Before the year was out, the sixteen-year-old Sammon, renamed Peggy Shannon, on the strength of six weeks' rehearsing with the chorus line, was on stage in the 1923 edition of the *Ziegfeld Follies*. Other jobs followed in quick succession, including a stint with Earl Carroll's *Vanities* revues in nightclub floorshows. At Texas Guinan's Hippodrome she shared the spotlight with another up and comer, Ruby Keeler, and by 1927 was on Broadway as the ingénue in *What Ann Brought Home*. Shannon went to Hollywood and in 1931 was billed as the next Clara Bow in *The Secret Call*. When the film opened in Pine Bluff in July, the mayor issued a "Peggy Shannon Day" proclamation.

But soon it ended badly. Shannon made too many bad movies too quickly (fourteen between 1931 and 1933), attempted a Broadway comeback in 1934 (in *Page Miss Glory*, with newcomer Jimmy Stewart), and ended up back out west in losers like *Youth on Parole* (1937) and *Girls on*

*Probation* (1938), in which her role as an inmate named Ruth is uncredited. By 1941 she was dead, at the age of thirty-four; her husband returned from a fishing trip to find her at their kitchen table, dead for twelve hours, cigarette still in her mouth. Three weeks later the widower shot himself in the same chair. "I am very much in love with my wife, Peggy Shannon," his note read. "In this spot she passed away, so in reverence to her you will find me in the same spot." Not a good end, though there are worse. At least somebody loved her too much to contemplate living without her.

Betty and Evelyn Francisco, born in Little Rock, worked in Hollywood in the 1920s and 1930s. Betty (1900–1950) began by saving a tenderfoot actor from real cowboy trouble in *A Broadway Cowboy* (1920). Though rarely receiving high billing, she worked steadily into the next decade, with roles in more than sixty films, including two of Harry Langdon's now-classic silent comedies, *The Strong Man* (1926) and *Long Pants* (1927), as well as Cecil B. DeMille's second sound film, *Madam Satan* (1930). Sister Evelyn (1904–1963) started later and stopped earlier, appearing in just over twenty films from 1924 to 1929, many of them uncredited shorts in which her role is often billed as "Bathing Beauty" or "Dancing Girl."

Janet Chandler (1911–94), born in Pine Bluff as Lillian Elizabeth Guenther, also worked in Hollywood in the 1920s and 1930s, appearing in a dozen films. Several are westerns—her performance in *Cowboy Holiday* (1934) can still be seen online.

Another dancing Arkansan whose fame derived in part from the movies was Irene Castle, though she was far better known as a ballroom dancer and dance instructor in company with her English husband, Vernon Castle. The two were international dance stars, and Irene in particular became a fashion trendsetter, credited with popularizing bob hairstyles and jeweled headbands. At the Café de Paris, the Castles introduced Europeans to various ragtime dances—

Peggy Shannon.

Betty Francisco.

Evelyn Francisco.

Janet Chandler.

their foxtrot was especially famed. Back in New York the couple took Broadway by storm, starring in *Watch Your Step* (1914), with a score written for them by Irving Berlin. They also produced a bestselling dance-instruction book, *Modern Dancing* (1914), lavishly illustrated with themselves in action, and starred as themselves in 1915's *Whirl of Life*.

Vernon served as a fighter pilot in World War I but died in a 1918 crash while training American pilots in Texas. From 1917 to 1922, Irene made nearly twenty films and served as an advisor for the 1939 biopic *The Story of Vernon and Irene Castle*, starring Ginger Rogers and Fred Astaire, which she disliked both for its falsity and for the producers' refusal to allow an African American actor to play their African American employee (the studio chose Walter Brennan). Topping off these many triumphs, Castle designed the Indian Head logo for the Chicago Black Hawks NHL hockey squad (her third husband, coffee baron Frederic McLaughlin, owned the team).

Castle chose Arkansas as home after visiting her son in Eureka Springs in 1954. She lived there, devoting herself to gardening and animal welfare work, until her death at seventy-five in 1969. Recent scholarship has stressed the Castles' efforts on behalf of African American music—they traveled with an African American orchestra and issued records by the Castle House Orchestra, led by composer-director James Reese Europe.

Surely the first-generation Arkansas actress with the longest career in film is Little Rock–born Alma Mabel Conner (1927–). She went to Hollywood as child actress Ann Gillis (sometimes Gilles), appearing first as an uncredited extra in *Men in White* (1934). Her last film role came thirty-four years later, in 1968, in Stanley Kubrick's *2001: A Space Odyssey*. Memorable roles in between include the part of Becky Thatcher in *The Adventures of Tom Sawyer* (1938) and the title role in the same year's *Little Orphan Annie*. Gillis is also the uncredited voice of Faline in the iconic 1942 animated film version of *Bambi*.

This adds up to a pretty impressive cohort of Arkansas actresses in a fledgling industry. After Broncho Billy, however, the state's next real star would be the versatile Dick Powell (1904–1963), who started as a boyish crooner in 1930s musicals before going on to even greater success as a jaded tough guy in 1940s noir films. Powell was born in Mountain View and also lived in Berryville and Little Rock before launching his show-business career as a vocalist, banjo player, bandleader, and theater emcee in Kentucky, Indiana, and Pennsylvania. He recorded steadily for Gennett (an Indiana label), Vocalion, and Brunswick from 1927 to 1930 before breaking into movies as a singing band-leader in *Blessed Event* in 1932. A string of hit musicals followed, most notably 1933's classic *42nd Street*, Powell's fifth film, a mix of Busby Berkeley's lavish dance numbers and Lloyd Bacon's gritty, halfway-to-noir narrative. In all of these Powell played a bubbly youth—"I'm Billy Lawler, one of Broadway's better juveniles," he says, introducing himself to newcomer Peggy, played by Ruby Keeler.

*42nd Street* made Powell a star, and he spent the next decade crooning and dancing his way through two dozen musicals, from *Footlight Parade* of 1933 and 1936's *Stage Struck* through the patriotic extravaganza *Star Spangled Rhythm* in 1942. (He also played Lysander in a 1935 version of *A Midsummer Night's Dream*, the only Shakespearean role of his career.) In 1935 he did a film remake of *Page Miss Glory* one year after the Broadway version featured an already downbound Peggy Shannon, while in *Star Spangled Rhythm* Powell shared a crowded stage—"More Stars Than the American Flag!" claimed the studio trailer—with new star Alan Ladd. Arkansas seemed well represented, in Hollywood and on Broadway, as the Depression gave way to World War II. And for Powell in particular, an already impressive career in musicals behind him, a major change was in store.

Broncho Billy's western heroics were by this time long ended;

Dress worn by Irene Castle, c. 1925.

Irene Castle.

Dick Powell.

*Uncle Tom's Cabin, Hallelujah,* and *Gone with the Wind* had claimed their place in cinematic history; and *42nd Street* and its sequels successfully transplanted the backstage musical's combination of spectacular Broadway production with strengthened narrative plotting to cinema. Flying far under this standard were Hollywood's initial forays into Arkie and Ozark stereotypes. Of the earliest numbers— *A Romance of the Ozarks* (1913), *Billie, the Hillbilly* (1915), *An Ozark Romance* (1918), and *Bishop of the Ozarks* (1923)—the less said the better. Harold Lloyd starred in *An Ozark Romance*— leave it at that. The high point of the first decades would likely be 1933's *Pilgrimage,* a dark, John Ford–directed tale of an Arkansas mother (effectively played by Henrietta Crosman) who sends her son to death in war to prevent his marriage.

The next decades would see new Arkansas cowboys as well as the first cowgirls, though Arkansas-born country-music star Patsy Montana actually claimed that title with her 1939 role in *Colorado Sunset,* with Gene Autry. Another Arkansas actress, who swam beautifully and looked good in a white swimsuit, would be menaced by a prehistoric monster in a pioneering 3-D picture. Arkansas musicians would continue to sing and play on the big screen (sometimes as cowboys), and new Hollywood films would make extensive use of the state's settings. Arkansans had played important pioneering roles in Hollywood's first decades. There would be more to come in the 1940s and 1950s.

# Tough Guys, Early 3-D, and a Sharpshooter in Pigtails

## *The 1940s and 1950s*

Broncho Billy and crooner Dick Powell were the state's brightest stars in Hollywood's first decades, joined by *Hallelujah* as the most significant shot-in-part-in-Arkansas film. The midcentury years would be headlined by angelic tough guy Alan Ladd and cowgirls Gail Davis and Dale Evans, he in hard-boiled roles, and they as sidekicks in Gene Autry and Roy Rogers westerns. The now less-boyish Powell would reinvent himself with spectacular success as a world-weary detective or insurance man, while William Warfield and Louis Jordan, working in very different musical traditions, would claim their own niches in Hollywood. Other successful Arkansans from these decades include singing cowboy Jimmy Wakely and versatile Julie Adams, who despite a lengthy career in both film and television was destined to be best remembered as the beautiful swimmer pursued by a prehistoric monster in *Creature from the Black Lagoon*, the pioneering 1954 3-D thriller. Lloyd Andrews, Jay C. Flippen, and Arthur Hunnicutt also made durable Hollywood careers in sidekick and character roles. The strongest claim for best shot-in-Arkansas film of the period would likely be 1957's *A Face in the Crowd*, one of the first serious portrayals of television's potential for demagogic misuse.

Powell transformed his career with a single movie, 1944's *Murder, My Sweet*, a film adaptation of Raymond Chandler's *Farewell, My Lovely*, which cast him as hard-boiled detective Philip Marlowe. A string of similar roles—in *Cornered* (1945), *Pitfall* (1948), and *The Tall Target* (1951), among others—highlighted Powell's mastery of the worn-down world of noir films, in which bad guys go down gruesomely and even good guys

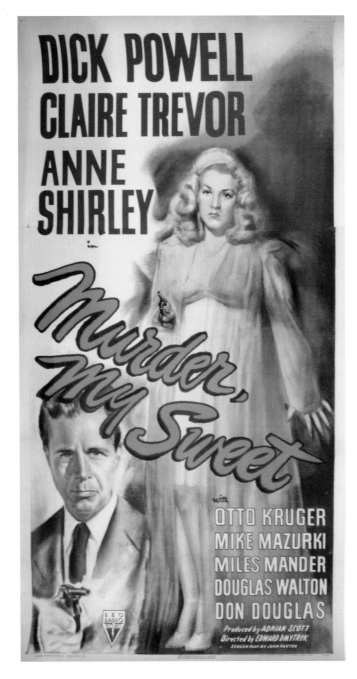

**DICK POWELL
CLAIRE TREVOR
ANNE
SHIRLEY**

in

*Murder,
my Sweet*

with

**OTTO KRUGER
MIKE MAZURKI
MILES MANDER
DOUGLAS WALTON
DON DOUGLAS**

Produced by ADRIAN SCOTT
Directed by EDWARD DMYTRYK
SCREEN PLAY BY JOHN PAXTON

earn the lumps they take on the way to the chastened enduring that passes for a happy ending. By the mid-1950s, Powell was busy primarily as a producer and director. His *Split Second* (1953) may be the first full-bore Hollywood feature directed by an Arkansan (Gilbert Anderson's films were shorter, and his work preceded Hollywood's rise). *The Enemy Below* (his 1957 feature), won an Oscar for special effects.

Today, however, Powell's directing career may be best remembered for *The Conqueror* (1956), a perennial contender for worst movie ever made. Starring John Wayne as (implausibly) Genghis Khan and Susan Hayward as the princess who comes to love the warlord who raped her (also implausibly), this lead-footed embarrassment was filmed on location in southern Utah directly downwind from the 1953 Nevada atomic-bomb tests at Yucca Flats, which irradiated the area's mostly Mormon and Native American citizens. The unsuspecting cast and crew of more than two hundred spent three months living, working, and breathing in the dust in one of the continent's most contaminated areas. Almost one hundred of those who worked on this film later developed cancer; nearly fifty died of it, including Wayne, Hayward, Agnes Moorhead, Pedro Armendáriz, and Powell.

Alan Ladd (1913–64) rose from humble and at times horrific beginnings to carve out a hugely successful career as a Hollywood megastar, though wealth and fame failed in the end to outweigh misery. Born in Hot Springs, he endured a childhood plagued by misfortune and poverty. His father died when he was four, and young Ladd soon after burned down the family's apartment while playing with matches. His mother then moved west to Oklahoma City and married an unemployed house painter, who relocated his destitute family to California in 1920. The son remembered the trek as something out of *The Grapes of Wrath*.

Ladd excelled as a high school swimmer and diver, though his dream of competing in the 1932 Olympics was dashed by injury. He struggled for several years after his graduation in 1934—he'd fallen several grades behind due to his family's lengthy travels and childhood illnesses caused by malnutrition—but found sudden fame in 1942 as a hired killer named Raven in *This Gun for Hire*. Other starring roles followed, including *Two Years before the Mast* and *The Blue Dahlia*, both from 1946, and the role of Jay Gatsby in a 1949 adaptation of *The Great Gatsby*. All these are major roles—if you are playing Jay Gatsby, you are the Redford or DiCaprio of your day. But Ladd's 1953 portrayal of the lone gunman Shane, who arrives, shoots the bad guys, and leaves to a boy's heartfelt call for his return, is generally regarded as his apex effort.

Directed by George Stevens (who would later do *Giant*) and costarring Jean Arthur (in her final film), Van Heflin, and Jack Palance in powerful supporting roles, *Shane* is often described, in company with

Dick Powell.

Alan Ladd.

Costume worn by Alan Ladd in *The Iron Mistress* (1952).

John Ford's *The Searchers* and a handful of others, as the greatest of Hollywood westerns. Both Woody Allen and Roger Ebert published tributes.

All in all, Ladd made some eighty films, often in pairings with top leading ladies like Veronica Lake (*This Gun for Hire*, *The Glass Key*, and *The Blue Dahlia*, among others), Olivia de Havilland (*The Proud Rebel*), and Sophia Loren (*Boy on a Dolphin*). He won awards, though never the biggest ones, and it took later scholars to find in his tough-guy roles a complexity worthy of analysis. *The Glass Key*, in particular, has been described by Gaylyn Studlar as offering Ladd's blonde good looks for homoerotic contemplation, meanwhile taking care to have the plot condemn such bonds as leading invariably to sadism. When Ladd's character (Ed Beaumont), attempting to infiltrate a gang, is beaten by a thuggish henchman (a very convincing William Bendix), the whole interaction is unmistakably sexualized. The thug introduces Ed at a bar with, "Meet the swellest guy I ever skinned a knuckle on." "What do you suppose gives me such a boot out of slugging you?" he asks. In short, Ed Beaumont is a gunsel, and there's every reason to believe author Dashiell Hammet knew exactly what he was doing when he created him. (He also snuck the often misunderstood word past uncomprehending editors and censors in *The Maltese Falcon*.) Strange currents are here, roiling under the shootouts and chase scenes.

For Ladd himself, stardom and the wealth that came with it weren't even close to enough. His first marriage failed. His mother, ravaged by alcoholism, killed herself by eating insecticide. The despondent star shot himself in a 1962 suicide attempt. Asked the year before what he would change in his life if given the opportunity, he gave a succinct answer—everything. In 1964, apparently accidentally, he finally burned the house down for good, this time by mixing alcohol and sedatives. Ladd was fifty.

Movies, like other forms of celebrity (sports, politics, and music), are a dangerous business for those at the top. *Hollywood Babylon* and its sequels continue to sell. But even in a field littered with contenders (including poor Peggy Shannon), Alan Ladd surely ranks as one of the unhappiest superstars of all time. In retrospect it seems somehow inevitable that, recovered from his thumpings in *The Glass Key,* he was flogged onscreen in *Two Years before the Mast* (1946) and *Botany Bay* (1948)—where he was also keelhauled—and some viewers have understood his character as fatally wounded as he rides stoically away at the end of *Shane*. Ladd's fame, however, abides—gawker tours still visit his Palm Springs home, and the first of the cat-o-nine-tails scenes enlivens the cover of a strange 2004 compilation aimed at a niche readership, *Lash! The Hundred Great Scenes of Men Being Whipped in the Movies.*

The story of Gail Davis (1925–97) is a happier tale. Born Betty Jeanne Grayson in Little Rock because her home town of McGehee then lacked a hospital, she studied drama at the University of Texas and got her breakthrough film role in the 1948 Roy Rogers western *The Far Frontier*. More skilled with horses than Bronco Billy, though famed stuntwoman Alice Van Springsteen doubled for her (and for Dale Evans) in trick-riding scenes, she proved an ideal cowgirl sidekick, eventually riding the range with stars like Johnny Mack Brown (in *West of Wyoming* and *Six Gun Mesa*, both from 1950) and fellow Arkansan Jimmy Wakely (in 1949's *Brand of Fear*). Above all, she worked in Gene Autry films, more than a dozen in all, beginning with *Sons of New Mexico* in 1949 and closing with *Pack Train* in 1953. Davis generally received third billing, after Autry and Champion, his horse.

Alan Ladd.

She also burnished her cowgirl credentials with television guest appearances on *The Cisco Kid*, *The Lone Ranger*, and of course *The Gene*

Gail Davis.

*Autry Show*, but Davis is best known today for her starring role as sharpshooter Annie Oakley in the 1954–1956 television series (the first female lead in a TV western), a role she also owed to Autry, whose company produced the show. Annie never killed anybody, specializing instead in disarming bad guys by shooting their guns from their hands. Davis's youthful audiences were both entertained and instructed—in "The Mississippi Kid," an episode from 1956, the pigtailed star (her contract with Autry forbade her to cut them) and sidekick deputy Lofty Craig manage to combine catching a gang of thieves with schooling a tenderfoot southern visitor on the virtue of modesty, the importance of asking for help, and the basics of gun safety. Davis's screen exploits earned a posthumous induction to Fort Worth's National Cowgirl Hall of Fame, and her Annie Oakley character has been described as a cinematic Nancy Drew, a dashing female star who encouraged her young fans to make for themselves a bigger place in the world.

If Davis has persisted in memory for *Annie Oakley*, just as Ladd is mostly remembered now for *Shane*, Arkansas's other film cowpokes from the 1940s and 1950s, Dale Evans (1912–2001) and Jimmy Wakely (1914–1982), are not so sharply identified with particular roles, though the Dale Evans–Roy Rogers film pairing, highlighted by their real-life marriage in 1947, was even more famous than the Davis-Autry tandem.

Born in Texas, schooled in Osceola, married at fourteen in Blytheville, and a mother in Memphis at fifteen, Evans struggled as an aspiring singer and actress until 1943, when she was paired for the first time with Rogers in *The Cowboy and the Senorita* (she was the senorita and sang "Besame Mucho" in convincing Spanish). It was the beginning of a spectacular run—the duo made more than thirty films together over the next decade, closing with 1951's *Pals of the Golden West*, just as their popular *The Roy Rogers Show* took off on television. They were Hollywood's top western-film couple, Rogers as "King of the Cowboys," Evans as "Queen of the West." Tie-in products included comic books and lunch pails for school kids. In the comic-book story "Jumbo on the Range!," Evans rides in pursuit of cowboy outlaws astride an elephant! Wildly far-fetched plots

Costume Worn by Gail Davis.

were standard fare. Autry's *The Last Round-Up* (1947) mixes a cattle stampede and an Indian uprising with a television broadcast, while his *Indian Territory* (1950, with Gail Davis) pits him as an Apache-speaking former Confederate officer against a rapier-wielding "renegade Austrian" villain nostalgic for his "castle on the Danube." Autry also finds time for a bunkhouse performance of "Chattanooga Shoeshine Boy," billed as a "boogie-woogie rag."

Evans and Rogers, who lost a two-year-old daughter to complications associated with Down Syndrome, adopted four special-needs children and worked to improve services for families of children with developmental disabilities. Evans's *Angel Unaware*, the first of several memoirs about her children, became a bestseller and an inspiration to other parents. She was also a high-profile Christian, rallying for school prayer, recording albums of religious songs, and in the 1990s hosting her own devotional television show, *A Date with Dale*. Her "Happy Trails," written as a theme song for their radio and televisions shows, has become something of a standard. Janis Joplin taped it just before her own death as a birthday greeting for John Lennon, and college bands sometimes play it at football games as a derisive send-off to vanquished visiting squads. Weird America lost a signature attraction when the Roy Rogers and Dale Evans Museum, featuring their stuffed horses Trigger (his) and Buttermilk (hers) and dog Bullet (shared) on exhibit, closed in 2009 after moving from its original Victorville, California, location to Branson, Missouri, where American kitsch goes to die. Evans also was inducted into the National Cowgirl Hall of Fame. Her good work on behalf of children continues via the Happy Trails Children's Foundation.

Gail Davis.

Dale Evans.

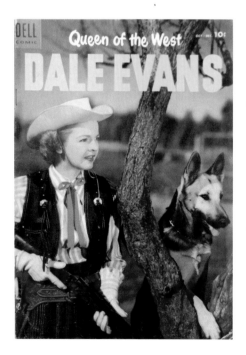

Jimmy Wakely (1914–1982) never achieved comparable fame or such association with a famous spouse-sidekick. Born in Mineola, he rose from humble Arkansas beginnings to appear in sixty movies, score country hits, and star in his own comic-book series. Wakely started as a country singer in Oklahoma City and made his film debut as an uncredited musician in *Saga at Death Valley* (1939), a Roy Rogers film. Before he hung up his spurs, he had sung with Gene Autry in *Heart of the Rio Grande* (1942), Tex Ritter and Johnny Mack Brown in *The Old Chisholm Trail* (1942) and *Tenting Tonight on the Old Camp Ground* (1943), and Hopalong Cassidy in *Stick to Your Guns* and *Twilight on the Trail*, both from 1941.

Wakely also prospered as a musician, twice making the top of the charts, first with "One Has My Name (The Other Has My Heart)" in 1948 and again with "Slippin' Around" the next year, a duet with Margaret Whiting that proved to be an even bigger hit (it also topped the pop charts). DC Comics produced a *Jimmy Wakely* series from 1949 to 1952, billing him on the covers as "Hollywood's Sensational Cowboy Star!" Well-preserved copies now command hundreds of dollars from collectors.

On the down side, Wakely also appeared in *I'm from Arkansas* (1944), a strong contender for low point in the crowded field of Ozark hillbilly comedies that succeeded the pioneering travesties of earlier decades. *I'm from Arkansas* is a wholly lamentable series of stereotyped Ozark gags attached to a preposterously incoherent plot, though some viewers might prefer even this to the saccharine redemptive-landscape bilge of *The Shepherd of the Hills* (1941). An even more egregious affront was *Child Bride* (1938), an early exploitation flick marketed as an "educational" effort to "help to abolish Child Marriage." This one has it all—pedophilia, moonshine, wife-beating, homicide—but it was filmed in California and never specifies even a regional locale for Thunderhead Mountain's "back yonder" hill folks.

Along with the cowboys and cowgirls, the state's best-known radio comics also went to Hollywood during these decades. Polk County natives Chester Lauck (1902–1980) and Norris Goff (1906–1978) had taken their Lum and Abner radio comedy show from its modest beginnings on Hot Springs radio station KTHS to the national networks almost a decade earlier, but in 1940, following in the pioneering steps of Bob Burns, they brought their Jot-Em-Down General Store to Hollywood for *Dreaming Out Loud*. Five more rustic comedies followed in short order, including *The Bashful Bachelor* (1942) and *Two Weeks to Live* (1943).

Arkansas musicians were no less successful. Louis Jordan (1908–1975) was an enormously popular bandleader throughout the 1940s, and William Warfield (1920–2002) was an internationally acclaimed concert bass/baritone who recorded with top orchestras and conductors and toured the world on behalf of the State Department. Neither was a cowboy (though Jordan donned a big hat and pistols for one of his roles), and movies remained at the periphery of their careers, but both made their mark in Hollywood.

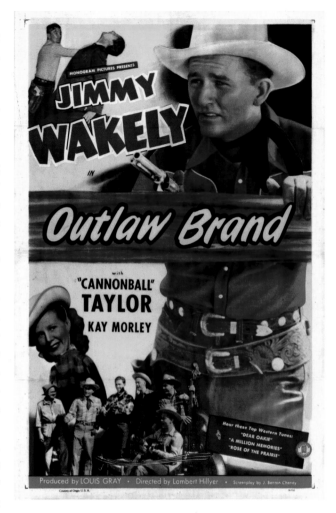

Born a musician's son in Brinkley, Jordan was playing professionally with his father as early as high school. He attended Arkansas Baptist College in Little Rock, and after a two-year stint with Chick Webb's orchestra at New York's Savoy Ballroom (Webb fired him for trying to hire his musicians away), Jordan assembled the first version of what would persist through many lineups of varying size as the Tympany Five. By the 1940s, when Hollywood called, the combo was hugely popular amid a

Louis Jordan.

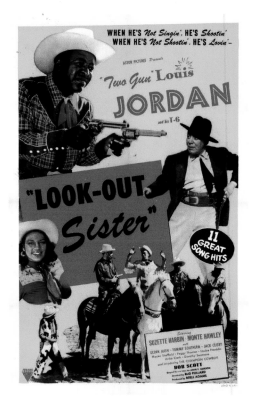

long string of now classic hits penned by Jordan himself (who also handled the vocals).

His early appearances included *Follow the Boys* (1944), a "cavalcade of stars" olio where he shared the stage with W. C. Fields and Artur Rubinstein, among many others, and *Swing Parade of 1946*, where he appeared with the Three Stooges. Jordan then moved quickly into the starring role, always playing himself and always playing his hits, in three "race" films—*Beware* (1946), *Reet, Petite, and Gone* (1947), and *Look-Out Sister* (1949). In the first his return to campus for a concert helps save his college from being closed by the founder's unscrupulous son (in real life Jordan provided financial support to Arkansas Baptist), while in *Look-Out Sister*, the strangest of the three, overworked bandleader Jordan is ordered to a sanatorium for rest and renewal and dreams himself to a ranch in Arizona threatened (like the college in *Beware*) by financial skullduggery. Togged out in a ten-gallon hat and holstered pistols, "Two-Gun Jordan and his Jivin' Cowhands" entertain guests and save the ranch, with Jordan waking up in time to help a young fellow patient realize his own cowboy dreams. The demise of the "race" film ended Jordan's career in Hollywood, but his musical career continued to flourish. "Saturday Night Fish Fry" was a number-one hit in 1949. Jordan was voted into the Rock and Roll Hall of Fame in 1987, twelve years after his death.

William Caesar Warfield, born in Helena, was just over a decade younger than Jordan, but his time in

Hollywood was even briefer. Except for an entirely forgettable minicameo in *Old Explorers* (1990), in which he does not sing, Warfield's only role in a feature film was Joe in *Show Boat*, the 1951 film version of the landmark 1927 Broadway musical. He made the most of it, claiming Jerome Kern and Oscar Hammerstein's already classic "Old Man River" as his own. He had big shoes to fill too—the 1936 version had featured Paul Robeson's rendition. Warfield's memoir, *My Music and My Life*, relates with considerable pride his one-take performance.

Warfield went on to a distinguished career, recording with top orchestras and conductors—including Handel with Eugene Ormandy and the Philadelphia Symphony Orchestra and Mozart with Bruno Walter and the New York Philharmonic—and starring as Porgy in a 1952 touring version of *Porgy and Bess,* with future wife Leontyne Price as Bess and Cab Calloway as Sportin' Life. He also played De Lawd in a 1957 television version of *The Green Pastures* and won a Grammy in 1984 for his narration of Aaron Copland's *A Lincoln Portrait*. But "Old Man River" and *Show Boat* remained his signature role—he was still singing the song on stage in Vienna as late as 1972.

Various 3-D technologies had been around almost since the beginning of movies, but a series of feature films from the 1950s are now regarded as a first "golden age" for the format, the first steps on the road to *Avatar*. Arguably the biggest hit in this initial flowering was the 1954 monster/horror flick *Creature from the Black Lagoon*, with Arkansan Julie Adams (1926–) as Kay Lawrence, a lissome marine biologist whose

William Warfield and Leontyne Price in *Porgy and Bess* (1959).

William Warfield.

graceful after-work swims in a sexy white suit attract the attention of a prehistoric amphibian "Gill Man." These cinematic dips also mesmerized a whole generation of smitten teenaged boys wearing their special glasses in theaters. The late Memphis musician Jim Dickinson remembered these scenes as "an unforgettable vignette in my early pursuit of happiness." An instant hit, the only 1950s 3-D film popular enough to spawn sequels (*Revenge of the Creature*, from 1955, and *The Creature Walks among Us*, from 1956), *Creature from the Black Lagoon* is available now in various formats for home viewing, including 3-D, amid rumors of a remake release.

Adams, born in Iowa as Betty May Adams and raised in Little Rock, had been in Hollywood since 1946 and appeared in some twenty films, mostly westerns, between 1949 and 1953. Credited as "Julia Adams" in her 3-D adventure, she would go on to a varied and successful career in both film and television, appearing in everything from the dark *Slaughter on Tenth Avenue* (1957) and Dennis Hopper–directed *The Last Movie* (1971) to the lightweight fare of Elvis flicks (1965's *Tickle Me*). Adams may hold the Arkansas record for sheer activity in the cinema business—her Internet Movie Database (IMDb) filmography listed 146 entries at last check. But even now she is remembered best for her underwater adventures in *Creature from the Black Lagoon*. The Gill Man has been good to her, Adams says, ever the gracious star willing to pose with fans and creature cutouts at conventions.

Stars, of course, are only the tip of the show-business iceberg—for every Dick Powell on the marquee or Peggy Shannon stepping onto red carpet for a glamorous opening, there are scores of less celebrated cast and crew members, comic sidekicks, and stunt riders tumbling from horses. Five Arkansans in particular made durable careers in such second-line roles in films of the 1940s and 1950s. The busiest of the lot was Nashville native Terva Gaston Hubbard (1902–1977), who as Trevor Bardette worked steadily in movies and television from 1937 to 1970, appearing in more than one hundred films in the 1940s alone. Mostly, he played bad guys and surely holds the Arkansas record for onscreen deaths.

Jay C. Flippen and Lloyd Andrews came to Hollywood from careers rooted in nineteenth-century urban and rural popular entertainments, while Arthur Hunnicutt worked first on stage and Dick Hogan started as a singer.

Flippen (1899–1971), born in Little Rock, was both precocious and versatile—working in blackface minstrel shows in his teens, on Broadway in his midtwenties, and by 1926, still under thirty, a headliner at New York's Palace Theater, the top of vaudeville's pecking order. He also made records and did sports broadcasts on the radio. In the late 1940s Flippen began working steadily in Hollywood, often playing either cowboy sidekicks or uniformed authority types (prison wardens, sheriffs, military officers). But here too he was a versatile actor who was up for anything. If he's the lawman up against bikers in *The Wild One* (1953, with Lee Marvin and Marlon Brando), he's no less at home in musicals (*Oklahoma!* and *Kismet*, both from 1955). In *Run of the Arrow* (1957), he plays a Sioux warrior named Walking Coyote; one reviewer called it almost a return to blackface.

Before he was through, Flippen did more than one hundred films and television

Scene from *Creature from the Black Lagoon* (1954).

Julie Adams.

shows, at least eight of them with Jimmy Stewart. At times Stewart must have wondered if he had moved to Arkansas—Julie Adams was his wife in TV's *Jimmy Stewart Show*, Peggy Shannon shared the stage in his Broadway debut in *Page Miss Glory*, and Anthony Mann's western *Bend of the River* (1952) featured Stewart with both Adams and Flippen. Flippen's long and varied career continued almost to his death—he lost a leg when his diabetes worsened during the filming of *Cat Ballou* (1965) but turned in a scary bit part as a wheelchair-bound political boss in 1971's *The Seven Minutes*. He died that same year.

Where Flippen prepped for Hollywood mostly in vaudeville's and Broadway's urban settings, his near-contemporary fellow Arkansan Lloyd Andrews (1906–1992) arrived via a very different and less lucrative path. Born near Gravette, his career as an entertainer started in traveling tent shows and other rural entertainments. Andrews was a gifted if unconventional musician who specialized in playing everyday objects as instruments, and he toured the South and Midwest for years as a one-man band, a hawker of tonics, and a slapstick comedian in the "Toby" banjo-comic tradition—bare feet, exaggerated freckles, red-haired wig, and blacked-out teeth. When he married in 1929, his wife, Lucille, joined him on the road.

Andrews went to Hollywood in 1939 after Tex Ritter saw his show in Monticello, Arkansas, and promised to help if he would journey west. *Rhythm of the Rio Grande* (1940) was the first of ten Ritter-Andrews pairings. Billed most often as "Arkansas Slim" (he was six feet, eight inches tall), he was often mounted on a mule named Josephine. Andrews appeared in other sidekick roles—he made more than twenty films between 1940 and 1952—before moving into children's television in the

1950s as the sun set on singing-cowpoke films. His best role may have been in *Take Me Back to Oklahoma* (1940). Andrews eventually returned to Arkansas, commuting to his final children's TV shows in Pittsburg, Kansas.

Arthur Hunnicutt (1910–1979) worked neither vaudeville nor tent shows, but he too was a great success in Hollywood. Born in Yell County's Gravelly community, he embarked on a stage career when he couldn't afford to finish college. He was on Broadway by 1940, toured as the country rascal Jeeter Lester in a stage adaptation of Erskine Caldwell's *Tobacco Road*, and appeared in the first of some fifty films (and nearly as many television shows) in 1942, often playing a rustic cowpoke named "Arkansas." Even as a younger man, Hunnicutt made his living playing grizzled oldsters, most famously as Uncle Zeb Calloway in *The Big Sky* (1952), which earned him a Best Supporting Actor Oscar nomination. Hunnicutt appeared with the period's biggest stars, supporting Kirk Douglas in *The Big Sky*, Audie Murphy in *The Red Badge of Courage* (1951), and John Wayne in *El Dorado* (1966). He played Davy Crockett in the 1955 Alamo flick *The Last Command* (Sterling Hayden starred as Jim Bowie), worked with fellow Arkansan Jay Flippen in *Cat Ballou*, and also appeared in *Split Second* (1953), Dick Powell's directing debut.

Little Rock native Dick Hogan (1917–1995), the youngest of the five, worked as a vocalist with Glenn Miller's orchestra before breaking into films in the late 1930s and working steadily, if often in uncredited roles, through the next decade. He appeared with Humphrey Bogart in *Action in the North Atlantic* (1943) and with fellow Arkansas Alan Ladd in *Beyond Glory* (1948). Hogan's last film was the Alfred Hitchcock murder mystery *Rope*, also from 1948.

In 1957, Hollywood returned to Arkansas for the shooting of *A Face in the Crowd*, the first significant film shot in the Natural State by a noted director since *Hallelujah*. Elia Kazan had something to prove, and Andy Griffith was taking his first shot at a big role. Kazan had caved to Senator Joseph McCarthy's House

Jay C. Flippen.

Lloyd 'Arkansas Slim' Andrews.

Arthur Hunnicutt.

Un-American Activities Commission witch hunt in 1952, as had screenwriter Budd Schulberg, and now that McCarthy had fallen, both were often derided as craven snitches.

In *A Face in the Crowd,* Kazan explores very similar issues by creating an environment in which demagoguery thrives and power mongers bend an eager-to-be-manipulated public to their will. The film serves as a prescient glimpse into how television and other media can be used to both create and destroy demagogues, sweeping good (if strikingly gullible) people along in their wake until a crack in the façade exposes the frightening reality just beneath the surface. But this powerful film, boasting an impressive cast, made little impression at the box office and met with mixed reviews. More recent critics, however, have noted both the originality of the movie's insights and its important place in the history of film. In an interview for the supplements to the film's 2005 DVD release, Jeff Young, author of *Kazan: The Master Director Discusses his Films*, calls *A Face in the Crowd* "the most important and most underrated film of the twentieth century."

Cast members Patricia Neal and Walter Matthau were anything but faces in the acting crowd at the time, but Lee Remick and Anthony Franciosa were relative newcomers, and Griffith, the central face of the film, was making his first feature. Based on Schulberg's short story "Your Arkansas Traveler," the movie focuses on the metamorphosis of a down-at-the-heels singer and yarn spinner into media celebrity "Lonesome" Rhodes (Griffith). Encountering him first in a local jail's drunk tank, radio journalist Marcia (Neal) encourages him to sing on the air, telling her small-town Arkansas audience that most of the world's talent is out there with the common folk. Rhodes is happy to oblige, belting out "I'll Be a Free Man in the Morning." Even before he leaves the cell, he demonstrates his gift for engaging his audience, but he also proves a quick study who first apprehends the power of electronic media through his appearances on the local show that gives the movie its name.

Rhodes possesses all the traits later seen in Sherriff Andy Taylor of the famed *Andy Griffith Show* just three years later—he has an easy smile, exudes warmth, tells downhome stories, and strums his way into the hearts of his listeners. But where Taylor's warmth is genuine, Rhodes's is wholly false, a façade deliberately contrived to make money and wield power. Lonesome Rhodes is Andy Taylor with an added dash of sociopath and egomaniac.

Both radio and television allow Rhodes to reach mass audiences. On the first he bonds with local homemakers, encouraging them to send him pies and give him their allegiance, which he readily puts aside as soon as a better deal comes along. On television he's a mattress salesman and pitchman for Vitajex, an energy tonic that's only real claim is that it won't hurt anybody. As he boards the train for Memphis and future fame, he shouts out to the hundreds from Pickett (read "Piggott"), Arkansas, gathered at the station to see him off, "I'll be thinking about you good people."

But then, as the train pulls out, he drops the folksy mask: "I'm glad to shake that dump," he says. Marcia is shocked, and Rhodes retracts the remark, but it's a preview of what's to come—and of a much more public statement he will not be able to undo. The film's viewers watch,

fascinated and appalled, as Rhodes moves ever upward, from small town to big city to Big Apple. But he is not content with just singing songs and spinning yarns. "I am not just an entertainer; I am an influencer; a force, a force," he proclaims.

And this remains true as he improves the approval rating of an unappealing pol in the race for president from less than 5 percent to over 50 percent. His manipulation of his now 65 million viewers disgusts those who see behind the curtain, and it horrifies Marcia, his business partner, long-term friend, and sometime lover (when Lonesome is especially lonesome). She's the one who eventually pulls the curtain aside (by turning the mike on) so his public at last sees what Lonesome really thinks of "those morons out there." In Schulberg's story Rhodes dies instead, falling down a long staircase in sexual pursuit of "Marshy," his dark side never revealed. His death is a good career move, enhancing his image and sealing his fans' affection for him permanently.

But there is no final good career move for Lonesome in the film.

He begins his trek to stardom and power with a song, "Free Man in the Morning." But he's never in fact free, caught up as he is in a meaningless rhetoric that he does not believe, deployed to attract the allegiance of a mass audience he scorns. At the end of the film he is ranting in the cadences of a preacher (making good use of Griffith's seminary training) to an audience of one. He's now the only one fooled, the man in the dark, with only an applause machine to keep him company.

As the 1960s dawned and Hollywood films moved into their second half century at the center of the nation's entertainment industry, *A Face in the Crowd* stood out as a striking exception. Arkansans had mostly found places for themselves in front of the camera. Gilbert Anderson was the state's first director as well as its first star, but he did his pioneering work in the days before Hollywood's emergence. Dick Powell's work as a director, even aside from the tragic fiasco of *The Conqueror*, is largely a footnote to his durably successful acting career. The state itself had by any measure a modest presence as a location for movies—*A Face in the Crowd* was the only major-studio feature shot primarily in Arkansas, though the apparently now lost *Wonder Valley* (1953), shot in and around Cave Springs, was big news when it premiered in Bentonville. *Uncle Tom's Cabin* and *Hallelujah*, major films with important scenes shot in Arkansas, would tie for the second spot, with the don't-blink-or-you'll-miss-it minicameo in *Gone with the Wind* filling out the roster.

All this would change in the next two decades. The state would continue to provide its share of actors and actresses (and at least one celebrated stunt man), but the 1960s and 1970s would also see several Arkansas directors make their mark, and the number of films shot at Arkansas locations would see a sharp surge.

# TAKE THREE  True Grit, Fake Monsters, and Many Explosions

## *The 1960s and 1970s*

An actor, not a director, led Arkansas filmmaking into the 1960s. Johnny Cash (1932–2003), the Man in Black, already a Sun Records recording star with big hits to his singing and songwriting credit (including "I Walk the Line," "Folsom Prison Blues," and "Hey Porter"), made his Hollywood debut in 1961 in *Five Minutes to Live*. He's the lead, playing Johnny Cabot, a sadistic gunman redeemed only by a weak spot for children (he apparently shot one by mistake in a prior heist). "I'm a killer," he tells his banker's-wife hostage. The film itself is silly enough, a black-and-white mashup of noir (a gangster narrator whose confession frames the story) and sitcom elements (a *Leave It to Beaver* domestic scene, with the kid thwarting the bad guys by faking his own death and his dad's impulse to run off with a mistress stifled when he's reawakened to his love for his wife by the threat to her life). But Cash is effectively creepy, veering oddly between strumming his guitar, destroying furniture, waving his gun around, and eroticizing the whole scene with recurrent suggestions of both rape and/or rough sex. "I like a messy bed," Cabot says. The role showcases Cash as the same hard man who cut the coldest version of "Delia" ever—"hard to watch her suffer, but with the second shot she died."

Ten years later Cash would play a tough gunman again, this time in *A Gunfight* (1971), with Kirk Douglas and Karen Black (and a bit part by newcomer Keith Carradine). The plot centers on a winner-take-all showdown in a bullring (we're to view the scene as a New World gladiatorial Coliseum), but it's really a vehicle for a machismo display condemned

Johnny Cash in *Five Minutes to Live* (1961).

by the narrative and celebrated by everything else. Carradine, Cash, and Douglas are all impressively menacing, and the film itself rates a notch or two above the genre average.

Cash does not appear (he had been dead for two years), but Joaquin Phoenix stands in for him in *Walk the Line* (2005), a compelling account of the singer's struggle with his brother's early death and the hostility of an abusive and bitter father, leading the son to drug and alcohol abuse. Cowritten by Gill Dennis and director James Mangold, the film makes June Carter as interesting a figure as Cash. Reese Witherspoon garnered a Best Actress Oscar for her portrayal of Carter, and both actors do a great job delivering the music.

Cash was not alone in carrying forward the tradition (already well established by Powell, Warfield, Wakely, Jordan, and others) of Arkansas musicians acting in films. Smackover-born rockabilly legend Sleepy LaBeef (1935–) also took to the screen, rampaging as a Louisiana swamp monster in the unimaginably lame *The Monster and the Stripper* in 1966, six years before *The Legend of Boggy Creek* made its Arkansas cousin, the Fouke Monster, famous in drive-ins across the land.

Hat worn by Johnny Cash in *A Gunfight* (1971).

*True Grit* is Arkansas's most famous film. Based on the novel by El Dorado native Charles Portis (1933–), the movie is set largely in the state, and the 1969 version marks the Hollywood debut of Delight native Glen Campbell (1936–). It is certainly the only Arkansas-based film to enjoy both a sequel (1975's *Rooster Cogburn*) and a remake, with star-studded casts in all cases. But the movies carried an importance to Arkansans beyond their ability to draw crowds and make money. Set in the 1880s in Dardanelle, Fort Smith, and the Indian Territory (modern Oklahoma), the story celebrates the fierce character of the state's people through admiring depiction of its young heroine, Mattie Ross. H. L. Mencken might report that, coming back from a tour of the country "lying along the border between Arkansas and Oklahoma" was like "emerging from a region devastated by war. Such shabby and flea-bitten villages I had never seen before, or such dreadful people." But Portis's work provides a more balanced portrait of the same country, putting forward a heroine insisting on "true grit" as an admirable trait of its people.

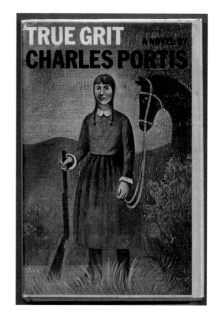

In 1969 Arkansans could believe their state had arrived as they watched the iconic John Wayne play Rooster Cogburn, a role that earned him a Golden Globe and his only Oscar. Never mind that Cogburn is a U.S. marshal far beyond his prime who likes "to pull a cork" and often ignores legal niceties, killing bad guys he might have tried a little harder to deliver alive to Judge Parker's rough justice. This is John Wayne after all, a tough, straight-shooting, all-American guy (personal life and social attitudes aside), won over by a fierce young girl (Kim Darby) looking to bring her father's murderer to justice.

This first *True Grit* sets its tone with the voice of Glen Campbell singing its theme—find a man with true grit and your pain will ease. But the movie goes beyond this claim; audiences find a girl who not only possesses true grit herself but who also brings out the same quality in those who throw in with her. In those first moments, as Campbell croons, the camera focuses on "480 acres of good bottom land on the south bank of the Arkansas River not far from Dardanelle in Yell

Glen Campbell.

County." It is lovely, but Arkansans were surely surprised to see a Yell County with snow-capped mountain peaks (the Rockies) in the background.

Other liberties mostly accommodate the star power of Wayne: Cogburn cannot die at the end, he must instead jump a fence and ride off into the distance, his death a thing for the future. And Mattie cannot be permanently maimed through her association with him—though she loses her arm in the book, in the first film version, her arm is simply in a sling with the promise of full recovery. By the end all the villains—including a young Dennis Hopper as Moon—are dead. Of the good guys, only Texas Ranger La Boeuf (Campbell) dies, but he perishes heroically, saving the lives of Mattie and Cogburn. La Boeuf lives in the book, but the change leaves Cogburn/Wayne as the only hero left standing. One day in the distant future, Cogburn will rest for eternity on the Ross farm, buried with the closest thing he has to a family. Though screenwriter Marguerite Roberts made major changes in the plot, she wisely understood that Portis's narration and dialogue couldn't be improved, and so much of it remains, often word for word.

Despite fond memories of seeing the first *True Grit* in Fort Smith at about Mattie Ross's age with a father who raised quarter horses, admired John Wayne, and clearly thought the film potentially instructional for his book-absorbed, horse-fearing daughter, that daughter nevertheless prefers the 2010 Coen brothers' version. The setting, though filmed in Texas and New Mexico, is truer to Arkansas and Oklahoma landscapes. The script sticks more closely to Portis's original, and the dialogue flows more naturally. The Coen brothers' film is darker, more threatening, and its Mattie (Hailee Youngfield) seems younger and even more remarkable. She is a willful child who sharply instructs an adult neighbor, an undertaker, a horse trader, a boarding house operator (played by Fort Smith native Candyce

Hinkle), and various lawmen on the proper discharge of their duties, but she is also ready to charge bravely and uncomplainingly into dangerous country, chasing men who will not hesitate to kill her.

The 2010 version also strays at times from Portis's plot, but such changes always serve to underscore Mattie's fiercely independent character. She goes to a hanging in Fort Smith on her own, without her neighbor Yarnell, whom she has already "dismissed" back to Yell County with her father's body. And this time it is Mattie, not La Boeuf, who climbs the cabin roof to smoke out Moon and Quincy.

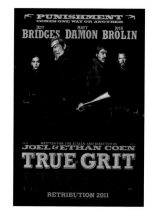

Jeff Bridges's performance as Rooster Cogburn is convincing, though unlike Wayne, he did not win an Oscar (despite ten nominations, the film came up empty). Bridges's Cogburn is part lawman, part outlaw, and part reprobate, but over the course of the film, we watch his attachment and respect for Mattie develop. The more he cares about her, the more we like him. This film also lets us meet the grown Mattie. Still fierce, she is a self-described one-armed spinster who does not worry much about what her neighbors think. She never sees Cogburn again after the night he saves her life, but she eventually buries him on her farm, ignoring as a grown woman the same raised eyebrows she brushed aside as a child, as determined upon gratitude and loyalty toward the man who saved her as she was upon justice toward the father who raised her. In both films it's Mattie Ross who both embodies "true grit" in herself and insists upon it in the conduct of others. Her twice-told saga adds up to the state's greatest portrait in film.

Portis was not alone among Arkansas authors in seeing his work adapted for the screen. Maya Angelou (1928–) saw her best-selling memoir from 1970, *I Know Why the Caged Bird Sings*, turned into a made-for-television movie in 1979. Dee Brown (1908–2002) didn't live to see it, but his great *Bury My Heart at Wounded Knee* (1971) also made the small screen in 2007. Bill Harrison (1933–2013) turned his 1973 *Esquire* short story, "Roller Ball Murder," into *Rollerball*, a 1975 film starring James Caan. Harrison's *Burton and Speke*, from 1982, was the source for *Mountains of the Moon* (1990), and Bette Greene (1934–) had her young-reader classic *The Summer of My German Soldier* (1973) adapted for television in 1978. Joe Klein (1946–) wasn't from Arkansas, but the subject of his anonymously published *Primary Colors* (1996) certainly was, and the 1998 film that followed was a blockbuster, earning two Oscar nominations (Elaine May for the screenplay and Kathy Bates for Best Supporting Actress); Billy Bob Thornton also appears as James Carville. And surely the record for longest-delayed film adaptation for an Arkansas author would be the German *Die Goldsucher von Arkansas* (*The Arkansas Gold Rush)*, a 1964 treatment of Friedrich Gerstäcker's 1845 *Die Regulatoren in Arkansas* (*The Arkansas Regulators*), now recognized as an early instance of the western genre. *Die Goldsucher von Arkansas* was released under several titles in Europe (and as *Massacre in Marble City* in the United States).

If *True Grit*'s varied Arkansas connections provided a fine Arkansas sendoff for 1960s movies, the following decade would distinguish itself by the arrival of the state's first cohort of directors. Four in particular stand out: three for personal ties to the state and one for the choice of Arkansas shooting locales. James Bridges was born in Paris (Logan County), while Charles Pierce and Harry Thomason were next-door neighbors as boys growing up in Hampton—Thomason was born there; Pierce moved in

James Bridges.

from Indiana as an infant. Roger Corman, the most prolific of the four, famed both for churning out no-budget B movies that made money and for giving future A-list stars and directors their start, was born in Detroit in 1926 but used Arkansas locations for both *Bloody Mama* (1970) and *Boxcar Bertha* (1972).

Corman and Pierce were committed mavericks who operated outside Hollywood and in conspicuous violation of mainstream cinematic pieties, but Bridges (1936–1993) in particular made his way in more conventional fashion, heading straight to Hollywood after studying drama at Arkansas State Teachers College (now the University of Central Arkansas). He started out in television, gaining his first success as a scriptwriter—his adaptation of Ray Bradbury's "The Jar" for *Alfred Hitchcock Presents* earned him a 1963 Emmy nomination. Bridges broke into directing in 1970 with *The Babymaker* and had his first major hit three years later with *The Paper Chase*, which won John

Houseman an Oscar for Best Supporting Actor and garnered two other nominations (including one for Bridges's adapted screenplay).

A long string of hits followed. *The China Syndrome* (1979) featured an all-star cast (including Michael Douglas, Jane Fonda, and Jack Lemmon) narrowly averting catastrophe by exposing corrupt mismanagement of safety standards in a nuclear power plant. It earned four Oscar nominations, including Bridges's second for Best Screenplay. Other blockbusters include *Urban Cowboy* (1980) and *Bright Lights, Big City* (1988). But it is his second feature, 1977's *September 30, 1955*, that is most deeply rooted in his Arkansas experiences. Both written and directed by Bridges and filmed on his old college campus in Conway, the film chronicles the reaction of a group of college friends to news of movie idol James Dean's death in a car crash. With rabid Dean fan and campus football star Jimmy J in the lead, the group's attempts at appropriate memorial observance lead to an end very nearly as grisly as Dean's own. The closing has Jimmy motorcycling out of

town, his football days behind him and Dean's big shoes beckoning to his future. *September 30, 1955* has long been noted as the screen debut of actor Dennis Quaid, but it also marked the first film role for Fayetteville native Lisa Blount, then a seventeen-year-old student at the University of Arkansas. She too would go on to big things.

Harry Thomason (1940–) also made it to the top in mainstream entertainment, though his triumphs were centered in television rather than movies, and his path was more convoluted than Bridges's. Following stints as a high school teacher and football coach, he broke into films in 1973 with *Encounter with the Unknown*, three tales of mayhem, madness, and ghostly return linked by a spooky Rod Serling commentary. Two years later he resurfaced with *So Sad about Gloria* (lots of blood in darkened houses, with at least three axe murders) and *The Great Lester Boggs* (motorcycle and car wrecks, a rodeo and a bar fight, explosions, and Alex Karras as a bumbling sheriff). Following two more B-movie efforts in 1979—*Revenge of Bigfoot* and *The Day It Came to Earth*—Thomason moved into television as a producer with *The Fall Guy* and the 1982 miniseries *The Blue and the Gray*.

Little Rock and central Arkansas are all over both the movies and the TV shows. *The Great Lester Boggs* (still available as *Redneck County*) includes Beebe locations, Mount Holly Cemetery is featured in *Encounter with the Unknown*, and even the mostly wretched *So Sad about Gloria* is redeemed by the appearance of Dionicio Rodriguez's North Little Rock *faux bois* concrete sculptures. *The Blue and the Gray* was shot entirely in Arkansas, with President Lincoln (Gregory Peck) delivering his 1861 whistle-stop speech in Eureka Springs instead of Leaman Place, Pennsylvania, and John Brown's 1859 trial occurring in Judge Parker's Fort Smith courtroom in place of Charles Town, Virginia (now West Virginia). Carnall Hall, on the University of Arkansas campus in Fayetteville, shows up in a bar scene, and then–Razorback athletic director Frank Broyles appears in a grim cameo to announce Lincoln's death.

Thomason and his spouse, Linda Bloodworth-Thomason (they married in 1983, with the Memphis Symphony Orchestra supplying music) struck television gold in the 1980s, first with *Designing Women* (1983–1986) and later with *Evening Shade* (1990–1994) and *Hearts Afire* (1992–1995). She created the stories and wrote the scripts, he directed and produced, and together they cleaned up. Their next production starred Bill and Hillary Clinton—Thomason and Bloodworth-Thomason worked at the center of the presidential election of 1992, providing media advice and producing the campaign's biopic, *The Man from Hope*. More recent projects are returns to commercial work. Bloodworth-Thomason published a novel, *Liberating Paris* (still the Arkansas one), in 2004 (with plans for a film version apparently in the works as of 2014). Thomason meanwhile

directed a film about the final days of Hank
Williams, *The Last Ride,* in 2012. Like *The
Blue and the Gray,* it was filmed in Arkansas,
with Benton and North Little Rock standing
in for Tennessee, Ohio, and West Virginia.
Bloodworth-Thomason's latest effort is *The
Bridegroom* (she's both producer and direc-
tor), which premiered at the 2013 Tribeca
Film Festival, winning the Audience Award for
Best Documentary.

Charles Pierce (1938–2010) also took
a roundabout path to the movies, cover-
ing weather in Shreveport before going
into advertising and kids' TV in Texarkana.
Working with borrowed money, with screenwriting help from advertising-business friend
Earl E. Smith, Pierce used local citizens as
actors to produce *The Legend of Boggy Creek,* a
1972 pseudo-documentary about an Arkansas
Bigfoot known locally as the Fouke Monster
that reportedly menaced a family from the
small Miller County town in May 1971. Filmed
in the Texarkana area and costing less than
$170,000 to make, Pierce's debut effort proved
a hit with 1970s drive-in audiences and later
at-home viewers, ultimately bringing in close
to $25 million.

Still working with Smith, as he would throughout his career, Pierce
next produced *Bootleggers* (also filmed in Arkansas), a 1974 Ozark moon-
shiners comedy starring Slim Pickens and introducing future *Charlie's
Angels* star Jaclyn Smith. It failed to repeat its predecessor's success.
Following this, he made two 1976 westerns, *Winterhawk* and *Winds of
Autumn,* the former garnering a warmly supportive Roger Ebert review
and heralded by Pierce himself as ultimately generating a viewing audience equal to that of *Boggy Creek. Winterhawk* is an impressively ambitious

effort, aiming for lyric effects with slow-motion shots and extreme close-ups of horses moving across magnificent landscapes to tell a story in which, for once, the Indian is the star and not the sidekick, even if he's played by an Italian-American actor from Connecticut (Michael Dante). Even where the movie fails, it does so grandly, with an overstated scrolling introduction likening nineteenth-century Native Americans to "knights" and a piano score to accompany an austere, wintry film that would seem to demand deep strings or woodwinds. Years before the fanfare of *Dances with Wolves*, Pierce made extensive use of indigenous language. Fellow Arkansan Arthur Hunnicutt appears, along with a host of well-known western character actors (Leif Erickson, Denver Pyle, and Woody Strode among others).

In 1985, having no connection to an earlier *Boggy Creek* sequel, Pierce eventually produced his own follow up, *The Barbaric Beast of Boggy Creek, Part II* (1985). He wrote, directed, and starred as a University of Arkansas professor leading students in search of the beast. Pierce's son, who also appears in *Winterhawk*, plays one of the students. The Razorback football team makes a brief appearance.

When *Boggy Creek* hit, Pierce was already working in Hollywood, mostly in set design—his earliest credits included *The Sterile Cuckoo* (1969, with Liza Minelli) and *The Skyjacking* (1972, with Charlton Heston and Yvette Mimieux). He continued with this work, most notably with Clint Eastwood's *The Outlaw Josey Wales* (1976) and the still-engaging *Carny* (1980), with Gary Busey and Jodie Foster. But success also bumped him up to acting, writing, and directing, most notably in his third filmed-in-Arkansas work, *The Town That Dreaded Sundown*, a horror/slasher flick from 1976, his busiest year. Here Pierce, working again with Earl E. Smith, not only reprises the faux-documentary style of *Boggy Creek* to direct Oscar-winning actor Ben Johnson, but also casts himself as a bumbling policeman. *The Town That Dreaded Sundown* may now be best remembered for a gruesome scene in which the killer attaches a knife to a trombone's slide and slaughters his victim while playing the instrument.

Pierce is also listed as a writer on Eastwood's 1983 *Sudden Impact*—he's credited with Dirty Harry's now internationally famous line (Italian and Kenyan variants have been reported), "Go ahead—make my day." The phrase apparently originated back in Hampton. Unhappy with his son's delay in completing unassigned yard chores, Pierce's father told the boy at lunchtime that he was "gonna make my day" if the lawn wasn't mowed when he came home from work.

Combine Thomason's central Arkansas bloodbaths with Pierce's southwest Arkansas threats to public safety, and a state awash in B-movie gore and horror emerges, vivid instances of so-called exploitation films. But Roger Corman, the crowned king of this genre (he received an Academy Honorary Award Oscar in 2010), was in the state first, shooting his "based-on-a true-story" *Bloody Mama* in Yellville and other Marion and Baxter County locales. An outdoor party scene with traditional music and dancing includes old-time Stone County banjo player Bookmiller Shannon. At the center is Arizona "Ma" Barker (Shelley Winters), portrayed as dumping her hapless husband to lead her sons to spectacular deaths ending violent criminal careers. The boys (Robert De Niro and Robert Walden play Lloyd Barker and his brother, Fred) are both deviants, and their mother is no better. Frequent shots of breasts and butts punctuate the gunfire. Forty years later Walden, a long list of films (including *All the President's Men*) and television shows (such as *Lou Grant*) on his résumé, would return briefly to Arkansas to teach part time at the University of Central Arkansas.

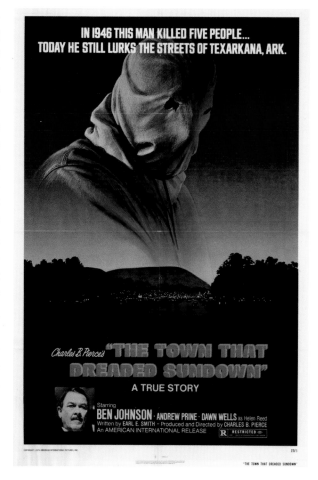

*Bloody Mama* was released in 1970. Corman was back the following year as producer of *Boxcar Bertha*, though this time Martin Scorsese directed. Barbara Hershey and David Carradine starred. Shooting centered in and around Camden, though Nevada County's Reader Railroad also makes an appearance. The story is loosely based on the "as told to"

autobiography of hobo and union activist Bertha Thompson published in 1937, with Carradine's "Big Bill" Shelly modeled on the flamboyant radical labor leader Big Bill Haywood. Again, there's plenty of gunfire and even more skin, with Ebert offering an appreciation of both in a nicely upbeat review.

Scorsese and De Niro are only two of a host of prominent directors and actors who got starts or boosts from the informal "Roger Corman Film School"—a partial list of others includes Peter Bogdanovich, James Cameron, Francis Ford Coppola, Peter Fonda, Monte Hellman, Dennis Hopper, Ron Howard, and Jack Nicholson. Fonda came to Arkansas to play family farm defender and Greenpeace-style ecowarrior Tom Hunter in Corman's *Fighting Mad* (1976), directed by Jonathan Demme and filmed mostly in Fayetteville and the nearby rural community of Wyman. Wilson Park hosts the assassination of a congressman, Fonda drinks beer in the old Swinging Door on Dickson Street, Zorro and the Blue Footballs make music, and University of Arkansas creative-writing professors Bill Harrison and Jim Whitehead enjoy thuggish moments on screen.

Hellman's apprenticeship with Corman started with *Beast from the Haunted Cave* (1959) and included uncredited editing to *Fighting Mad* as well as shared directing responsibilities for the now-legendary *The Terror* (1963), starring Boris Karloff. Corman himself is also credited along with Coppola, Nicholson, Jack Hill, and Dick Miller. Nicholson in later interviews defied anyone to make sense of its plot. The entertaining 2011 documentary *Corman's World: Exploits of a Hollywood Rebel* tells the story in full.

Hellman later included Little Rock and Faulkner County locations in his bleak and now much-lauded *Two-Lane Blacktop* (1971), with pop-music icons James Taylor and Dennis Wilson featured as younger, understated foils to a mesmerizing Warren Oates performance as the manic, middle-aged GTO. Unhinged by loneliness, desperate for any ear to hear his aggrandizing autobiographies, GTO screeches to a halt for every hitchhiker. "We'll build a house," he tells a bored, rootless girl (Laurie Bird), "because if I'm not grounded pretty soon I'm going to go into orbit." Near the end, after she's hopped a new ride, GTO spins yet another car-racing tale to just-picked-up soldiers. "That gives you a set of emotions that stay with you," he pontificates. "Those satisfactions are permanent." But it doesn't and they aren't, not for this character, not in this compelling film.

Arkansas is more central to *Wishbone Cutter* (1976). Directed by Earl E. Smith, taking time off from his collaborations with Charles Pierce, with Barbara Pryor as executive producer, this one is surely a serious challenger for the "released-under-most-titles" prize—there are at least eight in English (and it was also translated for European and South American audiences): *The Ballad of Virgil Cane*, *The Curse of Demon Mountain*, *Demon Mountain*, *Diamond Mountain*, *Shadow Mountain*, *The Shadow of Chikara*, and *Thunder Mountain*. Under whatever title, the movie was filmed entirely in Arkansas, mostly in Yellville (the old Cowdrey Mansion, which also shows up in *Bloody Mama*) and Marion County's Buffalo River country. It often succeeds despite a bizarre mix of staple elements. Opening as a Civil War film with Levon Helm's voice keening "The Night They Drove Old Dixie Down" on the soundtrack, it passes through western, bushwhacker, and treasure-hunt conventions before arriving at a supernatural-horror climax. Even today it has blogosphere enthusiasts, many having seen it first as youngsters on television.

*Smoke in the Wind* (1975), shot on location in Winslow with a screenplay by Fort Smith newspaperman and western novelist Eric Allen, was another story rooted in border-state violence in the post–Civil War era. The cast features Walter Brennan in his final feature role; his son Andy Brennan codirected with veteran Joe Kane (who apparently came out of retirement for his own last hurrah). But this film went nowhere very fast—not so much as a trailer seems to be currently available.

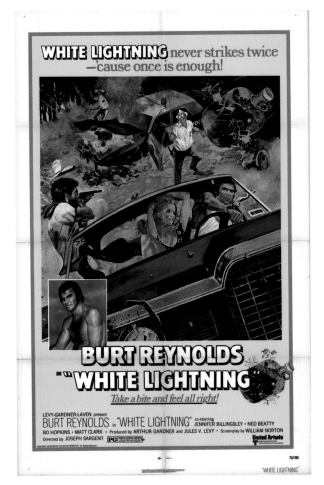

Arkansas locations, most centrally the Benton Speedbowl and the Tucker unit of the Arkansas State Penitentiary, are also prominent in *White Lightning* (1973), a Burt Reynolds vehicle also featuring fast cars and daredevil drivers. Reynolds was already a star (just one year earlier he'd appeared with Jon Voight in the Oscar-nominated *Deliverance* and with no clothes in a *Cosmopolitan* centerfold), but his spectacular success as moonshine runner Gator McKlusky launched a series of good-old-boy epics, most memorably *Smokey and the Bandit* (1977), well into the 1990s.

Arkansas connections in *White Lightning*, however, run deeper than shooting locations. A Honolulu-born graduate of Fort Smith High School, Jennifer Billingsley (1942–) stars as Lou, the girlfriend of Gator's fellow moonshiner Roy Boone, while Hal Needham (1931–2013), Reynolds's stunt double and longtime pal, was raised as an itinerant sharecropper's stepson in rural Union, White, and Phillips County communities.

Like many of her first-generation Arkansas predecessors in movies, Billingsley got her show-business start on Broadway, in the 1961 musical *Carnival*. She made her film debut in *Lady in a Cage*, a 1964 home-invasion horror flick starring Olivia de Havilland as a wealthy poet menaced by a gang of thugs. The film is terrible, though the trailer is hilarious, with de Havilland in her own voice presenting the carnage as a thoughtful exploration of home-security issues. Billingsley plays the top thug's sexpot girlfriend, a good prep for her role as "shaky pudding" Lou in *White Lightning*. Billingsley also appeared in several 1960s and 1970s films—*The Young Lovers* (1964), *C. C. and Company* (1970), and *The Thirsty Dead* (1976), among others—but was best known back in the day as Polly Prentice (1966–1967) on *General Hospital*, the long-running television soap.

Lee Purcell (1947–) was born in North Carolina but grew up in Paragould. Her first feature, *Adam at Six A.M.* (1970), with Michael Douglas, initiated a busy career in television and film. Like Billingsley, she appeared in many popular series—*Murder, She Wrote, Barnaby Jones, Marcus Welby, M.D.,* and *Due South,* among others—and earned two Emmy nominations for her performances in *Long Road Home* (1991) and *Secret Sins of the Father* (1994).

Hal Needham is even now not as widely known to moviegoers as the onscreen personalities or the directors, just as racecar mechanics enjoy less name recognition than the glamorous drivers, but in the world of stuntmen, he was the biggest name around. Born in Memphis, he came to Arkansas as a three- or four- year-old in the mid-1930s and left for St. Louis almost a decade later, wandering over a good bit of the state's rural outbacks in the intervening years as a down-to-the-bone sharecropper's son. Speaking to *Arkansas Times* writer David Koon in an extended interview seventy years later, he recalled those years as "not fun," noting that when he listed the towns his family lived in, he really meant they'd lived ten or twelve miles outside them, without electricity or running water. It was a very hardscrabble existence, though both the interview and Needham's rollicking 2011 memoir, *Stuntman!: My Car-Crashing, Plane-Jumping, Bone-Breaking, Death-Defying Hollywood Life*, are careful to credit it for his drive and work ethic. "One thing I learned in Arkansas was how to work," he wrote.

Needham prepped for his stunt career with work as a tree trimmer and a stint in the U.S. Army as an 82nd Airborne paratrooper. His first feature work involved hanging upside down from airplanes in the 1957 Lindbergh celebration *Spirit of St. Louis*, directed by Billy Wilder and starring Jimmy Stewart, but steady work came in the long-running television series *Have Gun—Will Travel*, in which Needham doubled for star Richard Boone and rose in a six-year stint from extra to stunt coordinator. His friendship with Reynolds developed when both men worked on NBC's 1959–1961 *Riverboat* series and led not only to *White Lightning* but also to the blockbuster *Smokey and the Bandit* and *Cannonball Run*

Hal Needham.

films. Hits with critics they were not, but ticket buyers loved them all; the box office for each was very good. Needham was still going strong as the twenty-first century rolled into its second decade, touring behind his memoir and being honored at the 2011 Little Rock Film Festival with a special showing of the original *Smokey and the Bandit* at Rivercrest Amphitheatre. There's also a fine NPR *Fresh Air* 2011 interview—it ran again after Needham's death in 2013 and is available online.

Other actors and actresses with Arkansas ties also made successful films in the 1970s. The most successful might be Hope native Melinda Dillon, who starred first on Broadway, earning a Tony Best Supporting Actress nomination for her portrayal of Honey in Edward Albee's *Who's Afraid of Virginia Woolf?* in 1962. By the end of the decade, she was in Hollywood (in *The April Fools*, from 1969), where she soon collected not one but two Best Supporting Actress Oscar nominations—first for *Close Encounters of the Third Kind* in 1977, then for *Absence of Malice* in 1981. From such early successes, Dillon went on to a durable career in film and television—from *Bound for Glory* in 1976 to *Reign over Me* in 2007, she played significant roles in impressive films. *Bound for Glory* won an Oscar for Best Cinematography, and Dillon picked up a Golden Globe nomination. Despite this imposing list, however, she's probably best remembered today for her 1983 role as Ralphie Parker's mother in *A Christmas Story*.

Fort Smith comedian, actor, and singer Rudolph Frank Moore (1927–2008) gained fame as Rudy Ray Moore, crossing over from spectacularly obscene comedy recordings of traditional "dozens" and "Signifying Monkey" toasts to films with the "blaxploitation" hit *Dolemite* (1975). Followed by a string of similar releases—*The Human Tornado* (1976), *Petey Wheatstraw* (1977), and *Disco Godfather* (1979)—*Dolemite* was described by *New York Times* critic John Leland as "the *Citizen Kane* of kung-fu pimping movies." Like Little Richard, with his claim to the title of "Inventor of Rock and Roll," Moore was not modest, billing himself as the "Godfather of Rap." Others have agreed—Dr. Dre sampled Moore's "Dolemite for President" on his 1992 album *The Chronic*, and Snoop Dogg contributed laudatory liner notes to the 2006 release of Moore's *Dolemite* soundtrack.

Two Little Rock actors also enjoyed long careers in television and film. Following college at Princeton, Ben Piazza (1933–1991) started on stage, landing his first Broadway role as George Willard in a 1958 stage version of *Winesburg, Ohio* and going on to much-praised performances in Samuel Beckett's *Endgame* (1962) and especially in three Edward Albee plays (*The American Dream* in 1962 and *The Death of Bessie Smith* and *The Zoo Story* in 1968). He made his first film in Canada in 1959 but was in good company in Hollywood the same year, appearing in *The Hanging Tree*

Melinda Dillon.

Ben Piazza.

with Gary Cooper. Piazza's 1970s films include *Tell Me That You Love Me, Junie Moon* (1970) and *I Never Promised You a Rose Garden* (1977), followed in the next decade by the likes of *The Blues Brothers* (1980), *Waltz Across Texas* (1983), and *Rocky V* (1990). The money was surely good, but at times such work must have seemed a long way down from Beckett and Albee. Piazza's last film was the 1991 *Guilty by Suspicion*, with Robert De Niro starring as a Hollywood director caught up in the Red Scare hearings.

Fellow Little Rock native Frank Bonner (born in 1942 as Frank Boers) is best remembered today as obnoxious sales manager Herb Tarlek in the CBS sitcom *WKRP in Cincinnati*, but he also forged a thirty-year career in Hollywood, appearing in ten features between 1970 (*Equinox*) and 1998 (*Motel*). Those numbers could jump to eleven and take the timeline past forty years if Bonner's latest effort, *Under the Hollywood Sign*, finished in 2012, is ever released. He also has worked as a director, mostly in television, with episodes of the Thomasons' *Evening Shade* and *Who's the Boss* among his credits.

Jonesboro-born Ben Murphy (1942–) grew up in Illinois, broke into Hollywood as a shaving college student in *The Graduate* (1967), and worked steadily for the next forty years, mostly in television. The high point of his career was a two-year lead role in *Alias Smith and Jones* in 1971–1972.

Two Arkansas actors also made names for themselves in outer space. George Takei (1937–) is best known for his nearly fifty-year television, film, and video-game turn as Hikaru Sulu, or Mr. Sulu as he is always called, in the varied iterations of the *Star Trek* phenomenon. Takei was born in California but spent a pivotal part of his youth under the guard towers at the Rohwer Relocation Center in Desha County, where he remembers learning the Pledge of Allegiance (his Arkansas experiences get two chapters in his 1994 autobiography, *To the Stars*). Takei's long and ongoing career rivals even Julie Adams's, his IMDb filmography listings pushing two hundred items. Among his recent projects is a stage musical, *Allegiance*, which enjoyed a lengthy run at San Diego's Old Globe Theater in 2012 and for which Takei has been leading a social-media fundraising campaign for a move to Broadway.

Gil Gerard (1943–) started out in Little Rock, not California, and went into space not on the Starship *Enterprise* but as Captain William "Buck" Rogers in the made-for-television movie *Buck Rogers in the 25th Century* (1979) and the subsequent television series (1979–1981). Both Gerard (in 2013) and Takei (in 2007) have appeared in the *Star Trek New Voyages: Phase II* series.

The 1960s and 1970s, viewed with hindsight's advantages, marked a turning point in Arkansas filmmaking, a two-decade period when, even as Arkansas actors built on the pioneering successes of their predecessors and continued to find their way to Hollywood, a cadre of directors (several of them native Arkansans) alerted the industry to the state's appeal as a location. If many of these films earned little in the way of critical praise, they regularly won approval at the box office. *Two-Lane Blacktop*, the best filmed-in-Arkansas piece from the period, was an impressive effort by any measure, but a host of others made elsewhere with Arkansans in prominent roles—including *The China Syndrome*, *Close Encounters of the Third Kind*, *The Paper Chase*, and *True Grit*—were all widely praised award winners. Even outliers like *Boxcar Bertha*, *September 30, 1955*, and *Winterhawk* have proved to have longstanding appeal.

By 1980, then, after a slow start in the previous decades, filmmakers worked on locations widely scattered throughout the state. Mostly, they were wrecking cars and making things explode. The formula developed by Roger Corman and carried to new levels of spectacle by Hal Needham was pretty straightforward. First, get good-looking actors and actresses and have them take their clothes off as often as possible. Second, get lots of machines (cars most of all, but also trucks, bulldozers, motorcycles, boats, and even airplanes) and crash them into houses, rivers, ponds, or each other until they won't run any more—then blow them up.

Thanks to their efforts, Arkansans became accustomed to seeing and reading about films being made in their midst, from Texas Ranger Ben Johnson chasing a killer in Texarkana to Peter Fonda taking out venal strip miners in Fayetteville and Burt Reynolds doing time in Tucker or driving recklessly in Benton.

All in all, the turbulent 1960s and 1970s were high times for Arkansas and for Arkansans in the film business. But even better was in store—blockbusters and Oscars in the offing—as the twentieth century headed into its final decades and a new millennium dawned. The second *True Grit* would be a highlight, Jeff Bridges stepping into John Wayne's oversize boots as Rooster Cogburn to reprise the tale of plucky Mattie Ross. Billy Bob Thornton would be as big in Hollywood as Dick Powell had been before, joining in various combinations with Jeff Bailey, Lisa Blount, Natalie Canerday, Rick Dial, Robert Ginnaven, Walter Goggins, Ray McKinnon, and Bill Paxton to form a rough cinematic equivalent of a theatrical repertoire company in producing a series of sometimes hilarious, sometimes harrowing, sometimes award-winning, but rarely all-the-way-cynical films. The directing triumphs of James Bridges would find worthy successors in the work of David Gordon Green, Jeff Nichols, and Derrick Sims. As the new millennium's first decade closed, a land-mark film set and filmed in Missouri would include a fine debut performance by a young Arkansas actress. Before that, the arrival of the 1980s would bring a perceptible acceleration in the state's cinematic efforts. Well-known directors and studios had by this time discovered Arkansas, and the state in turn, learning to appreciate the revenue filmmaking generated, was taking steps to make them welcome. The pace was picking up.

# TAKE FOUR   More Grit, Young Gun Directors, and Shelter Hard to Hold

## The 1980s to 2014

Three much-discussed films, all from the decade's opening year, gave Arkansas filmmaking a memorable introduction to the 1980s. First to arrive was *Coal Miner's Daughter*, the story of Loretta Lynn's rise from hardscrabble beginnings to country-music stardom. Released in March, it marked the cinematic debut of Turkey Scratch native Levon Helm (1940–2012). Helm, already well known as The Band's drummer, played the father to Sissy Spacek's Oscar-winning portrayal of Lynn. He'd go on to play a pilot in *The Right Stuff* (1983), a locomotive thief in *End of the Line* (1987, with Mary Steenburgen), an elderly bizarro in *The Three Burials of Melquiades Estrada* (2005), and rebel general John Bell Hood in the strange but compelling *In the Electric Mist* (2009, again with Steenburgen). The biggest loser on his résumé is surely *Man Outside*, released the same year as *End of the Line*, in which Helm appears as a not-too-bright sheriff with Band pals Rick Danko, Richard Manuel, and Garth Hudson in bit parts. This gobbler was filmed in Fayetteville, joining with *Fighting Mad* to make a formidable double entry in the "bad movie capital of Arkansas" sweeps. (The 1995 *Frank and Jesse*, with Rob Lowe as Jesse James and Randy Travis as Cole Younger, later gave a modest boost to the town's stock.) Helm also made a brief appearance in *Shooter* (2007).

*Brubaker*, released in June of the same year, was filmed in Ohio and featured no Arkansans, but its story was (loosely) based on Thomas Murton and Joe Hyams's *Accomplices to the Crime*, an account of Murton's

Levon Helm.

brief and tumultuous 1967–1968 tenure as a reform-minded warden of the notorious Tucker Prison farm, known at the time for a systematic, all-encompassing corruption and for a depraved cruelty boggling belief. (Look up "Tucker telephone" for details.) The screenplay earned an Oscar nomination, and Robert Redford starred as Murton, opening the film with a fictional undercover stint as a prisoner.

*Brubaker* is even now a harrowing film, featuring a young Morgan Freeman as a prisoner crazed by years without light in solitary confinement and a stunning last-bow cameo by Richard Ward as the lifer Abraham, who is dialed up a Tucker telephone "long distance call" to silence his story of the atrocities he has seen. Ward died in 1979, before the film was released; there's a tribute in the credit scroll.

*Melvin and Howard,* released in September, was the year's third Arkansas film, featuring Newport-born Hendrix graduate Mary Steenburgen (1953–), who won a Best Supporting Actress Oscar for her performance. With an infectious, dizzy energy, she plays stripper and quiz-show tapdancer Lynda Dummar, wife and then ex-wife of Utah filling-station owner Melvin Dummar, whose real-world claim to some $150 million via the so-called "Mormon Will" of billionaire genius and extreme recluse Howard Hughes was tossed by the courts in 1978. Jason Robards, terrific in his Hughes walk on, picked up a Best Supporting Actor nomination—Pauline Kael said he'd never been better.

Three films in one year, each an Oscar nominee, and each with ties to Arkansas. It was an auspicious start to the decade. *Melvin and Howard* was Steenburgen's third feature. She broke into Hollywood in 1978, opposite Jack Nicholson in *Goin' South*—she marries the rascal Henry Moon to save him from the gallows—and went on to a busy career in widely varied roles that continues today, most recently as a wryly generous, two-laps-around-the-block Vegas lounge singer who encourages Michael Douglas to grow up in *Last Vegas*, 2013's geriatric take on the *Hangover* series. In between are more than fifty films and nearly thirty television shows in which she plays everything from Richard Nixon's mother (in *Nixon*, from 1995) to struggling author Marjorie Kinnan Rawlings (in 1983's *Cross Creek*). Her performances in *What's Eating Gilbert Grape* (1993) and *Elf* (2003) have also been much praised. The latter is a better-than-expected Will Ferrell comedy, with Steenburgen playing a warmhearted wife who embraces her husband's out-of-wedlock adult elf. In the former she seduces the young Gilbert (Johnny Depp) in a still-impressive film that also features memorable performances by Darlene Cates and a pre-*Titanic* Leonardo DiCaprio (who picked up a Best Supporting Actor Oscar nomination).

Amid this impressive list, *End of the Line* stands out for its conspicuous ties to Arkansas. Produced by Steenburgen and written and directed by North Little Rock native Jay Russell (1950–), both children of railroad-worker fathers (who also make brief appearances), it was filmed on locations scattered across the state's central section (Benton, Little Rock, Lonoke, Pine Bluff, Scott) and in Chicago, with Steenburgen,

Mary Steenburgen.

Kevin Bacon, and fellow Oscar-winner Holly Hunter in supporting roles to Helm and Wilford Brimley. Governor Bill Clinton is thanked in the credits for his help, and like the Thomasons, Steenburgen became an active campaigner in the Clintons' 1990s presidential runs.

Russell, for his part, followed *End of the Line* with the film version of Willie Morris's best-selling memoir *My Dog Skip* (2000), where he again directed Kevin Bacon. Next up was *Tuck Everlasting* (2002), a Disney release starring Sissy Spacek. More recently, Russell received a "special thanks" credit for help with *Ain't in It for My Health*, the 2010 documentary portrait of Levon Helm.

Levon Helm, Mary Steenburgen, and Wilford Brimley, *End of the Line* (1987).

Fort Chaffee, already guaranteed a niche in pop photo lore for the 1958 shots of Elvis Presley's U.S. Army induction haircut, made Hollywood appearances in two military-themed films from the 1980s, *A Soldier's Story* (1984) and *Biloxi Blues* (1988). The biggest name from *A Soldier's Story* would now be Denzel Washington, but at the time he was a supporting player, moving up from his debut as an uncredited "alley mugger" in *Death Wish* (1974). The stars are Howard E. Rollins Jr. and Adolph Caesar, Rollins as a military lawyer investigating the death of Caesar as a boot-camp master sergeant. The place is Louisiana, the time is 1944, and the film itself is an adaptation of Charles Fuller's 1981 Pulitzer-winning drama, *A Soldier's Play*. Racial tensions are a central issue. The film was a critical success, earning Oscar nominations for Best Picture, Best Supporting Actor (Caesar), and Best Screenplay from Another Medium (Fuller). In addition to the central Fort Chaffee scenes, Clarendon streets were used as the fictional town of Tynin, Louisiana, and a baseball game sequence was filmed at Little Rock's Lamar Porter Field, with University of Central Arkansas players as the town squad. Music fans will enjoy Patti LaBelle as a joint singer named Big Mary (a clip can be found online).

*Biloxi Blues* is also a film version of a stage play. The middle third of Neil Simon's "Eugene trilogy," it opened in Los Angeles in 1984 and moved to a lengthy 1985–1986 Broadway run, picking up Best Play, Best Featured Actor, and Best Direction Tony awards along the way. Matthew Broderick and Christopher Walken star on both stage and screen, Fort Chaffee is again featured, and Van Buren stands in as Biloxi. Jeff Bailey (1956–) and Natalie Canerday make early appearances in bit parts—both would be heard from again.

The 1980s also saw the state capitol in Little Rock make it to the big screen as a double for the U.S. Capitol in the 1986 television movie *Under Siege*, best remembered today for what seems now a prescient anticipation of the 9/11 terrorist attacks. Hal Holbrook plays President Maxwell Monroe, with Edward G. Robinson as a senior advisor and Peter Strauss as an FBI agent urging restraint in reprisal attacks against Iran. Little Rock street scenes also appear, and Pinnacle Mountain State Park stands in for Maryland's Camp David presidential retreat. (Six years later Steven Segal

had a blockbuster hit with another *Under Siege*, this one featuring manly demonstrations of martial skills, a *Playboy* playmate, many explosions, and a narrowly averted nuclear-missile strike on Honolulu. Arkansas does not appear.)

If Arkansas filmmaking opened the 1980s with a bang, the end of the decade and the first years of the 1990s offered similar wealth. The luridly titled *Chopper Chicks in Zombietown* (1989) is a negligible effort, narrowly losing out in "worst movie with Arkansas ties" competitions to *The*

Billy Bob Thornton.

*Conqueror* as less pretentious and to *The Monster and the Stripper* for marginally higher production values. But it merits a hindsight footnote as an early appearance of Billy Bob Thornton (1955–), who already had *Hunter's Blood* (1986) and *South of Reno* (1988) behind him, and *One False Move* (1992) just ahead (with Jeff Bailey, Natalie Canerday, and Robert Ginnaven). He cowrote the latter with his friend Tom Epperson and shot part of it in Cotton Plant. In *South of Reno* (his second feature), Thornton crossed paths with a more grown-up Lisa Blount (1957–2010), who had been working steadily (mostly in television) since her teenage debut in James Bridges's *September 30, 1955*. The role of factory worker and flyboy chaser Lynette Pomeroy in *An Officer and a Gentleman* (1982) was her best-known performance in the interval, but Blount and Thornton would work together again almost two decades later in the powerful and still underappreciated *Chrystal* (2005), written and directed by Blount's husband, Ray McKinnon.

For Thornton himself, blockbuster success on three fronts (as writer, director, and actor) would arrive with *Sling Blade* (1996). Shot mostly in Saline County (Little Rock, Conway, and Clinton locations were also used), *Sling Blade* is a haunting and beautiful film with the unforgettable character of Karl Childers (Thornton) at its center. He's supported by a terrific cast—Lucas Black, Natalie Canerday, Rick Dial, John Ritter, and Dwight Yoakum (as a heavy) are all outstanding, and Robert Duvall is commanding in his two-minute solo. Fellow Arkansan Rick Dial (1955–2011), a Malvern native and long-time Thornton pal, is better-remembered today for *Crazy Heart* (2009) and *Bernie* (2011), but his *Sling Blade* performance as garage owner Bill Cox was his debut movie role. Thornton collected Best Actor and Best Adapted Screenplay Oscar nominations, winning in the screenplay category. He's been busy ever since, appearing in some forty films, racking up Oscar and Golden Globe nominations for *A Simple Plan* (1998) as well as Golden Globes for *Bandits* (2001), *The Man Who Wasn't There* (2001), and *Bad Santa* (2003). Though he did not receive awards recognition for his Hank Grotowski in *Monster's Ball,* Thornton turned in a powerful performance as did other members of the cast, including Heath Ledger, Peter Boyle, and Halle Berry (who received—and is still the only African American woman to ever win—an Oscar for Best Actress).

Thornton returned to directing with *Jayne Mansfield's Car* in 2012 and most recently gave an understated (for Thornton) but compelling performance in *The Judge* (2014) as Dwight Dickham, a district attorney determined to prosecute Joe Palmer (Robert Duvall), a local judge in Carlinville, Indiana. Palmer's estranged son (Robert Downey Jr.), a successful attorney, returns home for his mother's funeral and, as it turns out, to defend his father against a murder charge.

Other Arkansans who found success in Hollywood in the 1980s include actresses Tess Harper, born Tessie Jean Washam in Mammoth Springs, and Russellville native Natalie Canerday. Harper (1950–) made the biggest splash and got the earlier start, graduating from theme park roles at Dogpatch and Silver Dollar City to debut-year roles in two memorable films from 1983, *Tender Mercies* (with Robert Duvall) and *Silkwood* (with Meryl Streep, Kurt Russell, and Cher). She still tells interviewers that she started at the top and worked her way down. The slope was sometimes steep—the famously bad *Ishtar* was added to her résumé in 1987, and *Amityville 3-D* was a loser mixed in with the 1983 winners—but over time her ride was pretty much the standard win-some-lose-some roller coaster.

An obvious high point would be *Crimes of the Heart*

Lisa Blount.

Jacket Worn by Billy Bob Thornton in *Waking Up in Reno* (2002).

Tess Harper.

(1986). Working once again with an all-star cast—Diane Keaton, Jessica Lange, Sam Shepard, Sissy Spacek—Harper earned a Best Supporting Actress Oscar nomination for her portrayal of bitchy Chick Boyle, neighbor to the troubled McGrath sisters. The film itself deploys an astonishing range of dismaying southern stereotypes—think Tennessee Williams or the most overblown Faulkner played as farce. It's enough to suggest a rule of thumb requiring that region-centered films seek out homefolk directors—but Harper's was only one of its three Oscar nominations (the others were Spacek for Best Actress and Beth Henley for Adapted Screenplay). Her other winners would include *The Man in the Moon* (1991), *The Jackal* (1997), and *No Country for Old Men* (2007). Harper still lists the first as a favorite—Ebert's review was a straight-up rave.

Natalie Canerday (1962–), a Hendrix graduate, enjoyed her first role in *Biloxi Blues* in 1988, followed four years later by her first work with Thornton in *One False Move*. Her big hit was 1999's *October Sky*, with Jake Gyllenhaal and Chris Cooper, the story of a boy inspired by the Sputnik launch to build rockets in his hard-rock West Virginia coal town. Canerday also landed a lot of good work close to home, not only following up the *Sling Blade* triumph by working again with Thornton in *South of Heaven, West of Hell* (2000) but also appearing in Arkansas-born Jeff Nichols's first feature, *Shotgun Stories* (2007).

Four actors also forged varied careers beginning in the 1980s. Timothy Busfield (1957–) has been mostly a television actor, best remembered today for his Emmy-winning portrayal of Elliott Weston in *thirtysomething* (1987–91). His box-office successes include *Field of Dreams* (1989), *Revenge of the Nerds* (1984), and its 1987 sequel, *Revenge of the Nerds II*. Busfield's connections to Arkansas are slim—he spent two years at Conway High School in the 1970s.

El Dorado native William Ragsdale (1961–) has also made his career mostly in television—most memorably as

Herman Brooks in seventy-two episodes of *Herman's Head* (1991–94)—but he first came to fame as teen vampire fighter Charley Brewster in *Fright Night* (1985). Little Rock–born George Newbern (1964–) started in movies with *Woody* (1986) and has worked steadily ever since, compiling a résumé in film, television, and video games. His best-known roles are as Bryan McKenzie in *Father of the Bride* (1991, with Steve Martin and Diane Keaton) and its 1995 sequel, *Father of the Bride II* (with the same leading cast). Corin Nemec (1971–) broke in two years later in Francis Ford Coppola's *Tucker: The Man and His Dream* (1988), a heroized version of the story of Preston Tucker, the charismatic/catastrophic mix of auto-design genius and flimflam con artist responsible for the never-manufactured luxury auto that bears his name. Though Nemec went on to make other films in impressively varied roles, his busy career, like Ragsdale's, found its greatest successes in television. He's best known today for his leading role in the 1990–1993 teen sitcom *Parker Lewis Can't Lose*.

Natalie Canerday.

Jerry Van Dyke (1931–) came from Illinois and made a name for himself as Assistant Coach Luther Van Dam on the long-running (1989–97) ABC sitcom *Coach*. Marriage to Arkansan Shirley Jones brought him to a Hot Spring County ranch in the 1980s. In 1998 Van Dyke was inducted into the Arkansas Entertainers Hall of Fame. A soda shop bearing his name is still operating in Benton.

No Arkansans star in *Three for the Road* (1987), *Pass the Ammo* (1988), or *Rosalie Goes Shopping* (1989), but all were filmed in the state. The first, shot in Hot Springs and Little Rock, with Charlie Sheen in the top spot as a bad-guy politico's naïve aide, was a box-office dud and never released on DVD (though the full movie is available online). *Pass the Ammo* is a spectacularly uneven but occasionally quite funny spoof of a greed-head televangelist filmed on location in Eureka Springs (the Christ of the Ozarks makes an appearance). The over-the-top approach is perfect for the subject—is it possible to exaggerate the tackiness or the venality of these guys? *Rosalie Goes Shopping* is the best of the three, a wacky comic sendup of American consumerism. Rosalie Greenspace

It's not who you love.

It's how.

Ben Affleck
Joey Lauren Adams
Jason Lee

chasing
AMY

Finally, a comedy that tells it like it feels.

A film from the director of 'Clerks'

(Marianne Sägebrecht) is a German woman married to an Arkansas crop-duster pilot (Brad Davis) who wants only the best for her large family and gets it via an ascending array of financial maneuvers and scams. Her confessions to her priest (Judge Reinhold) are especially hilarious. Stuttgart and its surrounding rice fields are featured locations, but DeValls Bluff and Little Rock also appear.

North Little Rock native Joey Lauren Adams (1968–) arrived a bit later, breaking into Hollywood in 1993 with both *Coneheads* and *Dazed and Confused*. She has worked steadily ever since in both film and television, making her biggest splash as lesbian comic-book author Alyssa Jones in *Chasing Amy* (1997) but also appearing in *Mallrats* (1995), *Big Daddy* (1999), and *Trucker* (2008), among others. In 2006 Adams returned to Arkansas as writer and director of *Come Early Morning*, with Ashley Judd in the lead role (and Rick Dial in the cast). Shot on locations in Little Rock and North Little Rock, it was nominated for the Grand Jury Prize at Sundance, though box-office returns were disappointing. In her most recent Arkansas appearance, Adams stars in *Valley Inn* (2014), a romantic comedy written and directed by Arkansas native Kim Swink (1960–) and filmed in 2013 on location in Hindsville and Springdale. Natalie Canerday and Candyce Hinkle appear in supporting roles.

Jonesboro native Wes Bentley (1978–) also made it big in Hollywood in the 1990s, most notably as Ricky Fitts in *American Beauty* (1999). He went on to more spectacular success in *Ghost Rider* (2007) and *The Hunger Games* (2012), even as his triumphs shared headlines with reports of ongoing struggles with drug addictions. A Bentley film with a deep Arkansas connection is the straight-to-video potboiler *The White River Kid* (1999), a wildly incoherent, clumsily stereotyped attempt at comedy filmed in Hot Springs, Mount Ida, Petit Jean Mountain State Park, and other central Arkansas and Ouachita Mountain locations. The cast is better than the film, with Bentley in the title role accompanied by Ellen Barkin, Bob Hoskins, and Antonio Banderas in major parts. Randy Travis plays a corrupt sheriff, and presidential brother Roger Clinton makes a brief appearance.

Other Arkansans finding turn-of-the-millennium successes in Hollywood include Little Rock's Josh Lucas (1971–) and Fayetteville native Lauren Sweetser (1988–). After a decade spent mostly in television, including appearances with Nemec on *Parker Lewis Can't Lose*, Lucas made it big just one year after Bentley, playing an avaricious financier in *American Psycho* (2000) and a mathematician in *A Beautiful Mind* (2001). He's gone on to other widely different roles, starring as a maverick basketball coach in *Glory Road* (2006) and appearing more briefly as Charles Lindbergh in the Clint Eastwood–directed *J. Edgar* in 2011.

Sweetser's more recent notice, for her supporting role in the wonderful *Winter's Bone* (2010), may be as compelling as any Arkansas actor's break-in story. A 2006 graduate of Fayetteville High School, she was studying acting at Missouri State University when she landed a role in Debra Granik's film version of Daniel Woodrell's bleakly heroic tale of Ree Dolly's determined defense of her home and family. Cast as Ree's friend Gail, Sweetser holds her own, working with a stellar cast on a film as likely to endure as any with Arkansas ties. Jennifer Lawrence as Ree is a Missouri Mattie Ross, as bluffly commanding and even more heartbreakingly vulnerable. John Hawkes as her Uncle Teardrop builds a ragged ethic on a culture's ruins, then lives up to it. And Dale Dickey's Merab, chainsaw in hand, is perhaps the sharpest maternal image in a deeply feminist film.

The new millennium also brought to notice a surprisingly large cadre of young Arkansas-born directors. Earliest in point of time was David Gordon Green (1975–), born in Little Rock and raised in Texas. His first feature was the much-acclaimed *George Washington*, a visually gorgeous film

Jacket Worn by Joey Lauren Adams in *Chasing Amy* (1997).

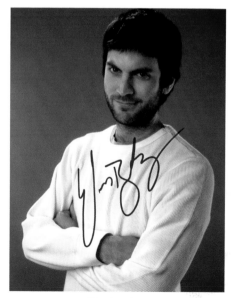

Wes Bentley.

Josh Lucas.

about mostly poor kids hitting adolescence in a hardscrabble North Carolina town where youthful dreams come up against hard realities way too soon. In *All the Real Girls* (2003), the cinematography is still stunningly beautiful. The kids are older, but times are still hard in North Carolina. Both films are slow paced and somber—we know right off we're watching a large talent. The same visual facility is present in smaller doses in the overblown thriller *Undertow* (2004) and in the bleakly compelling *Snow Angels* (2007), though almost wholly absent from Green's biggest hit, *Pineapple Express* (2008). The coherent explanation is box office—how else does so vapid a film come *after* works so commanding? (This explanation often serves—how does *Bad Santa* follow *Sling Blade?*)

Next to surface was Jeff Nichols (1978–), also from Little Rock and like Green a graduate of the University of North Carolina School of the Arts. Green, in fact, produced Nichols's first feature film, *Shotgun Stories* (2007), a riveting chronicle of a family divided by a nightmare father, an alcoholic whose three sons own generics for names—Son (Michael Shannon), Kid (Barlow Jacobs), and Boy (Douglas Ligon) Hayes. The film hints strongly that the first shotgun story occurs in a drunken outburst, with the unidentified father peppering Son, who is protecting his brothers, in the back with pellets. This event locks the brothers into their roles—Son as surrogate father, Kid as angry middle child, and Boy as obedient follower.

The only thing worse for these boys than their father is the mother (Natalie Canerday), who hates her ex-husband more than she can ever love her sons. She appears in only two scenes, and in neither does she connect in any way with her children. Her resentment for her ex-husband dominates, and it is unclear what she hates him for more, his abuse and abandonment of her, or the fact that he later found sobriety and Jesus and managed to put together a second family, with a wife and four sons he cared for and who cared for him.

The death of the father sets *Shotgun Stories* in motion. With him no longer around to absorb their anger, the older brothers turn their loathing upon their younger half-siblings. Unlike most epic battles pitting brother against brother, no land is at stake here, no kingdom, no right to rule, only memory, the matter of who has it right, who owns the story. Son's uninvited anti-eulogy at the father's funeral ends with him spitting on the casket, and so the feud begins.

A dirty-haired, heavily bandaged drug dealer named Shampoo (Alan Wilkins) connects the two camps, his gossip inciting all the ensuing violence. Soon one brother on each side is dead and another hospitalized. Only Boy, youngest of the older cohort, a hapless middle school basketball coach, is left to move the families toward resolution. He has a shotgun story of his own before the curtain falls. But he puts the gun down—critics who call *Shotgun Stories* a Greek tragedy miss the point. The movie ends with brothers left standing (or sitting on a porch), a sense of disaster narrowly averted, a modest hope for the next generation.

Jeff Nichols.

Nichols grew up in Arkansas—his grandparents lived in Altheimer, and he knows the towns of Scott, Keo, and England, where the movie was filmed. The images of small-town life in Arkansas are at times startlingly beautiful, slow paced, and forgiving, though the grasp on a decent life often seems tenuous. The threat of violence, rooted in old injuries, simmers beneath the placid surface. Though produced on a tight budget with help from family and friends (Nichols's musician-brother Ben is a major contributor here and in future films), *Shotgun Stories* is a powerful film carried by strong acting performances, especially by Shannon.

Nichols's next effort, *Take Shelter* (2011), centers on the psychological turmoil of Curtis LaForche (Shannon again). His oncoming illness expresses itself in anxiety over storms. This is, of course, not unreasonable

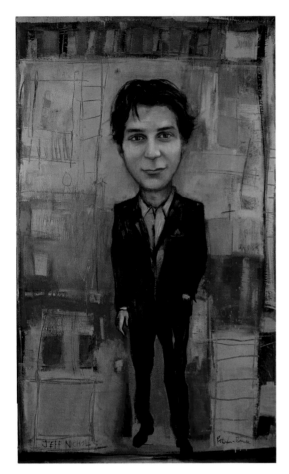

Jeff Nichols.

for a man living in the midwest, where tornadoes are a very real part of life, but the audience knows from the beginning that there is something different about Curtis's fears. The film opens (and closes) with a pending storm. In both cases the raindrops are brown, "The color of unused motor oil," he tells his wife, Samantha (Jessica Chastain).

Curtis begins having nightmares and hallucinations. He carries a sense of impending doom but wants desperately to protect his wife and his deaf six-year-old daughter. He checks out books on mental illness from the local library, sees a counselor, and eventually tells his wife what is happening. "You know where I come from," he says, referring to his mother, a paranoid schizophrenic who has been living in a mental institution since Curtis was ten.

But nothing helps lessen his fear of a cataclysmic storm, so Curtis builds an elaborate shelter in his backyard, a project that costs him his job, his best friend, and nearly his marriage. Nichols is very skillful in juxtaposing life's ordinary events with Curtis's extraordinary visions, making them all the more terrifying. We move from the water in the shower to the nightmarish storms of his dreams. Sometimes it is difficult for the audience to sort out what is real and what is imaginary. His nightmare becomes ours.

*Take Shelter* in some ways more convincingly portrays the terrifying descent into schizophrenia than the much celebrated *A Beautiful Mind* (2001). In that film John Nash eventually decides that three hallucinatory figures are not real because they do not age and is finally able to resume his life, teach, and be a husband and a father. But Curtis's predicament is more intractable—he cannot dismiss the storms as not real because sometimes they are, and at least once his shelter serves its purpose. The storm shelter is both a real and a metaphoric attempt to save himself and his family.

Finally, taking shelter from a storm proves easier than seeking shelter from a collapsing mind. At the film's end, the family takes a vacation to Myrtle Beach, a time to be together before Curtis begins intensive treatment for his illness. He looks out to sea, watches as a terrifying storm moves inland, and realizes, as the audience understands, that the truly terrible storm is the one in his mind. His wife looks at him knowingly, and the film closes with the family huddled together, hunkering down for the worst storm of their lives.

Nichols's third film is *Mud* (2012), the substance left after storms. Inspired by adding a personal take on *Huckleberry Finn* to his reading of *The Last River*, a photo collection documenting life on Arkansas's lower White River (which gave him at least the name and perhaps the character of the mussel diver Uncle Galen), he came up with a script Sam Shepard admired so much that he agreed to join the cast. The title works both as the name of the main character, a fugitive living on an island in the middle of the Mississippi River, and as a cue to the clarity of the film's ultimate answers to the questions it poses about love, honor, and family.

The action opens with two teenage pals, Ellis (Tye Sheridan) and Neckbone (Yell County native Jacob Lofland, in his first role), braving the open waters of the Mississippi to find a boat beached in a tree on an island. The fearless pair finds more adventure than expected. Ellis sees a cross, embedded in the heel of a fresh bootprint on the boat and knows his world has just been enlarged. More prints eventually lead them to Mud (Matthew McConaughey), a mysterious figure whose love for a troubled Juniper (Reese Witherspoon) will pull them into his story and make them willing partners in his quest to take the treed boat, make it seaworthy, and drift away from the world with his childhood sweetheart on board.

The boys soon find that like all quests, this one poses serious challenges. Mud is not forthcoming about his past—he murdered a man who beat Juniper and is now running from the law and the dead man's angry relatives. Ellis quickly adopts the Huck Finn attitude that he will help his new friend even if it is wrong in the eyes of the world. And help he does, taking notes to and absorbing punches for Juniper, bringing supplies to Mud, and finding castoff items useful in repairing the boat.

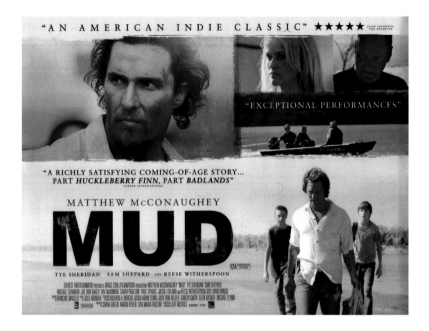

Ellis is desperate to believe in a love that overcomes obstacles because his own experience is pulling him in another direction. "You can't trust love, Ellis," his father counsels. "If you are not careful, it will up and run out on you." Ellis's own adolescent love for the fickle May Pearl seems to bear this out. He and Neckbone also watch a woman angrily exit Neckbone's trailer after Uncle Galen (Michael Shannon one more time) suggests an unwelcome bedroom activity as "Help Me Rhonda," Galen's "doing it" song, blares in the background. Ellis hopes for something more than Galen or his parents have, and Mud represents for him a love that endures through mistakes. That all this is spectacularly implausible, given Mud's name and circumstances, is exactly the point. Ellis is very young. Rebuilding the boat becomes a way to repair damage. The boat becomes for Ellis what the storm shelter is for Curtis—a tangible symbol of emotional aspiration.

Ellis doesn't have to overcome mental illness, but he does have to deal with a pair of lovers who have lost their ability to surmount the hardships they have inflicted on each other. The boy is furious when he thinks Mud has given up on Juniper. But in the end Mud rises to meet Ellis's standards, risking capture and even death to save his young friend.

Like all of Nichols's films, *Mud* ends on a subtle note affirming family life. Son and Boy sit, relaxed on the front porch, violence behind them, with Son's boy Carter, whose future may be less marked by violence. Even *Take Shelter*, the bleakest of the three, seems to offer the hope that Curtis, supported by his wife and daughter, may find some sort of shelter. *Mud* ends with two families rebuilding their lives. Ellis's father (Ray McKinnon) seems to have reconciled himself to a marriage with bridgeable differences, and Tom Blankenship (Sam Shepard) has once again saved Mud and overtly embraced him as his son.

Nichols's latest effort, *Midnight Special* (scheduled for release in 2015), is a science-fiction film that includes actors Kirsten Dunst, Michael Shannon (who else?), and Adam Driver. Once again the focus promises to be family.

Derrick Sims (1985–), born in Kingsland and educated at Henderson State University, is another important young Arkansas director. His darkly meditative *Come Morning* (2012) was filmed in various Cleveland County locations, including his hometown and New Edinburg. The story's center is a young boy, D (Thor Wahlestedt), drawn into a complex family land feud by a hunting-trip accident. But sinister intimations and strategic omissions run under the tightly plotted narrative to unsettle the viewer's urge to resolution. There's a woman in the house (Elise Rovinsky) whose relationship to the boy and to his grandfather (Michael Ray Davis) is left unclear. Morigan, an unusual name in a south Arkansas setting, is itself ominous. A figure by that name is a fearsome, shape-shifting battle goddess in the Irish Ulster cycle; her name translates as "Queen of Terror." The visual tapestry—stark, wet, cold—meshes perfectly with the narrative curve.

The newest kids on the young-director block are Daniel Campbell; the team of Christopher Thompson and Brian White; Juli Jackson; and David Hunt. Campbell (1981–), a Benton native schooled at Southern Arkansas University and UALR, has won an unprecedented three Charles B. Pierce Awards for best Arkansas-made film from the Little Rock Film Festival—the first was for *Antiquities* (2010), followed by *The*

*Orderly* (2011) and *The Discontentment of Ed Telfair* (2013). Engaging, offbeat jewels every one, they darken over time, from bashfully hopeful romance in the first, through comic defeat in the second, to murder by misunderstanding in the third (Jeff Bailey, in the title role, plays a strikingly hapless killer).

Thompson and White cowrote and codirected their debut effort, *The Gleaning* (2011), a mayhem-laced thriller set in the fictional town of Halcyon, Arkansas—"Hard to Find Harder to Forget"—and filmed in various locations around the state. It was screened at the Little Rock Film Festival in 2012. Jackson (1982–) returned to her hometown of Paragould to direct her first feature, *45RPM* (2012), a warmly comic road movie with an impressive list of 2013–2014 festival screenings (including Little Rock). After debuting with *Living Dark* (2013), a cave-exploration horror flick, Hunt turned next to *Greater* (2014), a feature-length biopic centered on the story of Brandon Burlsworth, a walk-on player for the University of Arkansas who was eventually drafted by the NFL.

Ray McKinnon came from Georgia, but he too directed several films with Arkansas ties. The first was the Oscar-winning 2001 short *The Accountant*, with his wife Lisa Blount as executive producer, followed by *Chrystal* (2004) and *Randy and the Mob* (2007). *The Accountant* is a small masterpiece, running less than forty minutes. It's as dark as comedy gets, the saga of a hayseed genius bookkeeper (played by McKinnon) with a preternatural facility with numbers. By your receipts he shall know you, this jalopy-driving, beer-swigging, pickled-egg-eating dark knight. And while he will save the family homestead from predatory corporate and banking interests, his price will be catastrophically high. By the film's close, he has assumed mythic stature, emerging as John the Revelator himself, come to write against your name. Title to property is made secure, even as hapless clients (played with clueless perfection by Walton Goggins and Eddie King) are left ravaged (and worse) by the unwelcome knowing he's imposed. Everything about this cold little beauty, from story to cinematography to soundtrack music, comes off as perfectly pitched. *The Accountant* would be an odds-on favorite for the title of most flawlessly executed film with Arkansas ties.

Filmed in Eureka Springs, and casting McKinnon with both Blount and Thornton, *Chrystal* eschews comedy for an aching story of injury, guilt, and chastened survival. All three are impressive in strikingly different roles—Blount so fragile she seems made of glass, McKinnon tightly wound and scary, Thornton consumed by old guilts and bent doggedly to atonement. It adds up to rough magic.

*Randy and the Mob* is lighter fare, a comic romp. McKinnon is terrific in two roles (small-town wheeler-dealer Randy and his gay brother Cecil), but Goggins often steals the show as a mob enforcer with really outstanding cooking and country-dancing skills. Blount is hilarious as Randy's wife, a baton-twirling teacher troubled by carpal tunnel syndrome. It's sometimes very funny—many a troupe would claim *Randy and the Mob* as their proud best, but *The Accountant* and *Chrystal* set very high bars.

The year 2007 also saw the appearance of *War Eagle, Arkansas*, a film with deep ties to the state. Based on a real-life friendship involving producer Vincent Insalaco's son, with a screenplay by Conway native Graham Gordy and filmed on locations in Eureka Springs, the film centers on the interdependent rela-

Lisa Blount and Ray McKinnon.

tionship of star high-school athlete Enoch Cass (Luke Grimes) and wheelchair-bound "Wheels" Macon (Dan McCabe). "Wheels" can't walk, and Enoch can't talk—he has a crippling speech impediment. The two are inseparable—together they have the small-town-skill-set spectrum covered. The crisis comes when a scholarship offer from a college in Tennessee presents Enoch with a stay-or-go choice. *War Eagle, Arkansas* won an impressive list of awards, including the 2008 Little Rock Film Festival's Charles B. Pierce Award.

No discussion of Arkansas filmmaking should close without mention of Phil Chambliss (1953–). A lifelong resident of the Camden area (claiming East Camden and Locust Bayou as home), Chambliss is about as far from Hollywood as it's possible to go, but he has recently

Lisa Blount.

become something of a favorite among indie-festival buffs as a cinematic "outsider artist." Beginning in the 1970s, supporting himself by a longtime job as a security guard for the Arkansas Highway Department and buying his first camera with funds saved to buy his ex-wife a refrigerator, Chambliss has produced some thirty films as a mostly one-man (writer, cameraman, director, editor) operation, casting local acquaintances as actors.

The films themselves are mostly shorts, with hand-lettered titles like *Shadow of the Hatchet-Man* (1982) and *The Mr. Visit Show* (2002), and only in the last decade have they been exhibited beyond the homes of local friends. The Nashville Film Festival gave Chambliss his debut public showing in 2004, and his films have since been shown to audiences in Memphis, San Francisco, and London. Attempts at description have been spectacular failures for the most part, though critics have come up with widely varied formulations. "Arkansas auteur" may be the most widely used, the Arkansas-French linkage apparently striking the aimed-for comic note. California managed "rural auteur" and practitioner of "red-state cinema," while the *Memphis Flyer* opted for "folk-art filmmaker," judged the "borderline-surreal" films as "so bad they're good," and pronounced one scene in *The Mr. Visit Show* "the most hilariously unstrenuous fistfight in movie history."

Recent years have also seen a surge of interest in community-based film festivals. Little Rock has celebrated theirs every spring since 2005, with steadily growing attendance and submissions. Currently administered by Arkansas filmmakers Brent and Craig Renaud (see Bonus Feature One), the week-long festival has been twice ranked among the nation's best. The Ozark Foothills Film Fest, held every fall in Batesville, has been going strong since 2002 under the dedicated care and direction of Bob and Judy Pest. Newer additions to the list include the Offshoot Film Fest in Fayetteville and the Eureka Springs Indie Fest.

From the meeting of Arkansas and Hollywood then—more than a

century of cinematic portrayals of a state more often scorned than praised, too often held up for ridicule in the nation's eye—what is an enduring image, a takeaway to cherish as counterweight to stereotype? Consider the sequence near the close of *Mud*, the fugitive named after wet dirt speeding by motorbike to the hospital, risking his freedom and his life to save the snakebitten Ellis. His is an errand of mercy; his needs give way to those of another. Notice then the eerie overlap with a similarly placed episode from *True Grit* (pick your version), sottish bounty-hunter Rooster Cogburn hurrying on horseback and then on foot to save snakebitten Mattie. These films run backward from 2012 (*Mud*) through 2010 (the remake of *True Grit*) to

Eagle carving from *War Eagle, Arkansas* (2007).

1969 (the first *True Grit*). Finally, leap back all the way to the beginnings, to Broncho Billy's 1915 silent short, *Broncho Billy and the Baby*. Here Billy's also a fugitive, and like Mud he exposes himself to capture or killing to rescue a child.

Three figures separated by a century, not one a community pillar, but each bent upon rescue, placing the welfare of another before his own. He's an archetype, this fellow, the despised figure from the margins who under pressure reveals unsuspected capacities for heroism and sacrifice. He is the scorned Samaritan who acts compassionately while priest and Levite pass by, the outsider hero of Paul Pena's wonderful song, "New Train": "the will of Christ is done by one from prison." As it happens, this figure also claims deep roots in Arkansas. He's celebrated by one of the earliest published Arkansas travelers, the German sportsman Friedrich Gerstäcker, who recorded his regret in his journal when after a five-year stay he left the state for the last time in the summer of 1842: "I may perhaps never see it again, but I shall never forget the happy days I passed there, where many a true heart beats under a coarse frock or leather hunting-shirt."

True hearts carrying on with true grit—this will do very nicely, won't it? So kick back and enjoy—visit the local multiplex or cue up one of Arkansas's films for company at home. Pop some corn, dim the lights, and hit play. True hearts in coarse frocks, guys from prison with names like Abraham, Shane, Gator, and Mud, young and old women from the hills named Mattie, Gail, and Merab. There they are, down on Arkansas ground, getting food to the table and keeping off the wind and rain, holding things together. There they are, up on Hollywood's big screen, rebuked and scorned, tattered and scarred, but acting as agents of mercy, insisting on justice, saving the homestead and looking after the children.

Roll the credits.

# BONUS FEATURE ONE    Documentary Film in Arkansas

Arkansas's pioneer documentary filmmaker was Freeman Owens. Serving with the U.S. Marines, first in Florida and later in France, he worked as both cinematographer and pilot on several propaganda films. *Flying with the Marines*, directed by pioneer theater owner and showman Samuel Rothafel, earned rave reviews at New York's Rivoli Theater (owned by Rothafel) in the summer of 1918. He also worked on *America's Answer: Following the Fleet to France* (1918) and *Devil Dogs at Belleau Wood* (1919). Out of uniform and back in the United States, Owens busied himself with additional documentary projects. *Race of the Age* chronicled the celebrated 1920 match between thoroughbreds Man O' War and Sir Barton, while the same year's *How Babe Ruth Hits a Home Run* focused Owens's newly invented slow-motion camera upon the Sultan of Swat's swing. Ruth was not amused, but his subsequent lawsuit was tossed, the judge ruling that as a public figure, the Babe could be photographed, even in slow motion, without his permission.

In the 1930s Arkansas was included in Pare Lorentz's classic cinematic hymn to the Mississippi, *The River* (1937). Lorentz made the film, and its no-less-distinguished predecessor *The Plow That Broke the Plains* (1936), under trying circumstances, harassed from nearly every point on the political spectrum. Hollywood studios, offended at his outsider impertinence, balked at supplying stock footage, actively hindered distribution of the finished films, and ruled *The River* ineligible for Academy Award consideration (it took the top documentary award at the 1938

Venice International Film Festival instead, beating out Leni Reifenstahl's *Olympia*). Congressmen suspicious of the very idea of government-sponsored films were doubly irritated by what they saw as pro-Roosevelt propaganda (they weren't wrong on that count) and as unflattering portrayals of their home districts. From the other camp, leftist camera crews were often mutinous over what they saw as Lorentz's refusal to condemn the destruction of the land by rapacious cotton planters and lumber barons.

Against such opposition, Lorentz held strong cards. One was the support of the Roosevelt administration, but his biggest assets were his own artistic sense and the striking talents of his coworkers. Virgil Thomson's score and Thomas Chalmers's narration are now recognized landmarks in their own right, while Lorentz's text, published separately, was nominated for the Pulitzer Prize in poetry. Leftists they may have been, but Willard Van Dyke, Stacy Woodard, and Floyd Crosby were spectacularly gifted cinematographers (Crosby had an Oscar to his credit). Arkansas's place in the film is centered in the penultimate section, documenting the devastating 1937 floods. Helena and Blytheville are named in the narrative.

A strong contender as a nascent Arkansas documentary filmmaking tradition's "unsung hero" would be Rogers native Jack E. Hill (1940–2012), whose groundbreaking role in promoting the genre in the state is still underappreciated. Trained as a journalist at the University of Arkansas and the University of Missouri, Hill capped off a decade-long stint as a television news anchor and star investigative reporter at Jonesboro's KAIT by moving to Little Rock, establishing his own production company, and producing more than fifty documentaries, mostly for the Arkansas Educational Television Network (AETN). Notable highlights among them are *Arkansas' Hemingway* (2003), an exploration of the ties between northeast Arkansas and the writing of *A Farewell to Arms; Before Little Rock: Successful Arkansas School Integration* (2007), a treatment of orderly public school integration in Charleston, Fayetteville, and Hoxie; and *Faces like Ours* (2009), a portrait of the internment of World War II Italian and German POWs in Arkansas prison camps.

Opportunities for statewide AETN broadcasts expanded in the 1980s under the direction of Raymond Ho and Mike Mottler. University of

Arkansas journalism professor Larry Foley spent nearly a decade at AETN in the 1980s and early 1990s and still cites Mottler as a mentor who taught him the business end of making films. Foley is best known today for the double Mid-America Emmy winner *The Buffalo Flows* (2009), the PBS-aired story behind the establishment of the country's first national river, though his work has focused on numerous Arkansas-based subjects, including *The Forgotten Expedition* (2002), a portrait of the pioneering Dunbar-Hunter exploration of the Ouachita River country and Hot Springs in 1804–1805, and (perhaps his personal favorite) *Charles Banks Wilson: Portrait of an American Artist* (2006).

Foley's University of Arkansas colleague Dale Carpenter also worked at AETN and trained his own lens upon Arkansas subjects. His 1998 *Broncho Billy: The First Reel Cowboy* is a documentary portrait of the state's first movie star, and *A Long Season*, his 1993 tracking of a Jacksonville Little League baseball team's season, proved so enduringly popular that PBS ran it in primetime for five straight years.

Arkansas's most celebrated documentary film project thus far is almost certainly the *Paradise Lost* trilogy produced for HBO over a fifteen-year period (1996–2011) by Joe Berlinger and Bruce Sinofsky. A harrowing tale of brutal murder, community hysteria, and legal/judicial malfeasance and incompetence in West Memphis, the 1996 *Paradise Lost: The Child Murders at Robin Hood Hills* provoked a national outcry and an organized movement on behalf of the three teenagers convicted (and in one instance sentenced to death) in what seemed to many viewers a conspicuous mockery of justice. The first film itself became part of the story in the second, *Paradise Lost 2: Revelations* (2000), and the third, *Paradise Lost 3: Purgatory* (2011). All three films were Emmy nominees, and the third earned a best documentary Oscar nomination. The same events are also treated in *West of Memphis* (2012), directed by Amy Berg, and most recently in the nondocumentary feature *Devil's Knot* (2014).

Brothers Brent and Craig Renaud of Little Rock have also produced award-winning documentaries, beginning with the Emmy-nominated *Dope Sick Love* (2001), a gritty, not-for-the-squeamish close-up of the lives of New York City heroin addicts, and following up with two Arkansas-based efforts, a ten-part series titled *Off to War* for the Discovery Channel in 2005, chronicling the deployment to Iraq of an Arkansas National Guard brigade, and *Little Rock Central: 50 Years Later* for HBO in 2007.

If Arkansas musicians found work in Hollywood from the film industry's earliest years, it's no less true that Arkansas documentarians have also gravitated to musicians as subjects. A pioneering effort was *The Search*, a 1954 made-for-television account of folksong research at the University of Arkansas led by English professor Mary Celestia Parler, featuring northwest Arkansas traditional singers Mary Brisco, Booth Campbell, Doney Hammontree, and Fred High. Huntsville rockabilly icon Ronnie Hawkins and son of Turkey Scratch Levon Helm have walk-on and central roles respectively in Martin Scorsese's much bally-hooed celebration of The Band's farewell concert, *The Last Waltz* (1978). Helm hated it, and while it's true that Scorsese's sycophancy and Robbie Robertson's narcissistic preening can nurture incredulity, the film still features genuinely powerful moments—Van Morrison, Muddy Waters, and the Staples. Louis Guida's *Saturday Night, Sunday Morning* (1992) has a primary focus on Memphis-based minister and ex-blues singer A. D. "Gatemouth" Moore, but the film includes good interview footage of Forrest City native Al Green holding forth on the incompatibility of Saturday's secular pleasures and Sunday's spiritual injunctions.

The traditional process of making maple syrup as practiced by Newton County resident Walter Williams is at the center of *Walking On* (1993), directed by Robert Cochran at the University of Arkansas's Center for Arkansas and Regional Studies in Fayetteville, with gospel-music performances by the Villines Brothers also featured. Western-swing fiddler and stonemason Frankie Kelly starred in the center's 1997 *Music's Easier*. Both films aired on AETN and are now archived in the Library of Congress's American Folklife Center in Washington, D.C. In 1998 Central Gospel Productions produced a two-disc set, *Living Legends of Gospel*, that includes a performance of "Count It as a Blessing" by the Dumas-based Racy Brothers (on disc one), and in 2007 Reelin' in the Years Productions released the wonderful *The American Folk Blues Festival: The British Tours, 1963–1966*. Several well-known musicians with Arkansas ties are featured—Sonny Boy Williamson and Howlin' Wolf among them—but the absolute showstopper is Cotton Plant's Rosetta Tharpe, buried in a bonus track. The footage must be seen to be believed—Tharpe performs in an outdoor train station during a rainstorm, wearing a heavy coat to protect her from the cold, separated from her audience by the tracks. Rising to the occasion, she opens with "Didn't It Rain," ends with "Trouble in Mind," and delivers a jaw-dropping, unforgettable show.

More recently, Augusta Palmer's *The Hand of Fatima*, a portrait of her father, Little Rock–born music critic Robert Palmer (1945–1997), was featured at the 2009 Little Rock Film Festival; Texarkana native Conlon Nancarrow (1912–1997), best known for his compositions for player piano, stars in James Greeson's 2012 *Conlon Nancarrow: Virtuoso of the Player Piano;* and the roots and variety of southern heavy metal music are explored in *Slow Southern Steel* (2011), directed by Christopher Terry. Levon Helm is front and center in director Jacob Hatley's intimate portrait *Ain't in It for My Health* (2010). He is pictured at home and on the road, still dancing thirty years after *The Last Waltz,* still nursing grievances over The Band's breakup, but cheered by the arrival of a grandson and Grammy-winning new work (three awards for three albums from 2007 to 2011) even as he struggles with the throat cancer that eventually would kill him.

Phil Chambliss makes films, not music, but when he appeared as the central subject of Simon Mercer's 2013 short, *Glass Eyes of Locust Bayou* (shown in the 2014 Little Rock Film Festival), he became the first Arkansas filmmaker featured in a documentary film (unless one counts *Corman's World* from 2011).

Documentary filmmakers in Arkansas have also turned their attention to the natural world and to the state's traditional culture. Fort Smith–born Marty Stouffer (1948–), creator of PBS's spectacularly successful *Wild America* program, would be the state's best-known wildlife filmmaker. His series ran for some 120 episodes from 1982 through 1996, producing along the way a number of spinoff videos (*Wild America: Dangerous Encounters* and *Wild America: Wacky Babies* give some idea of the range of these efforts) and a 1988 memoir, *Marty Stouffer's Wild America.* A closer-to-home effort is *The Hawks of Wilson Park* (2008), directed by Piggott native Carl Hitt (1947–), which follows a pair of red-shouldered hawks through three years of life in Fayetteville.

Doug Hawes-Davis's *The Naturalist* (2001) is a portrait of Buffalo River country outdoorsman and nature artist Kent Bonar, while Sarah Moore's *Witch Hazel Advent* (2013) focuses attention on Ozark homesteader and poet John Rule. *Bump* (2013), directed by Joe York for the Historic Arkansas Museum, is a beautifully made record of the split-oak chairs crafted by Dallas Bump and his family from Bear, in Garland County.

Finally, the documentary analogue of the Little Rock, Foothills, and Fayetteville Film Festivals would be the older and even better known Hot Springs Documentary Film Festival. Established in 1992 under the sponsorship of the Hot Springs Documentary Film Institute, the festival is recognized as one of the nation's most prestigious, screening dozens of new and old films at week-long programs and panels every October.

# BONUS FEATURE TWO  Picks and Pans

## TOP TEN FAVES

### ROBERT COCHRAN

*The Accountant*
*A Face in the Crowd*
*The Glass Key*
*Mud*
*Shane*
*Sling Blade* ✤
*True Grit* (2010) ✤
*Two-Lane Blacktop*
*What's Eating Gilbert Grape?*
*Winter's Bone*

### SUZANNE McCRAY

*The Accountant*
*The Big Sky*
*The China Syndrome* ✤
*A Face in the Crowd*
*George Washington*
*Sling Blade* ✤
*Take Shelter*
*Tender Mercies*
*True Grit* (both versions) ✤
*Winter's Bone*

## Very Honorable Mentions

*The China Syndrome* ✤
*Chrystal*
*Five Minutes to Live* ✤
*42nd Street*
*Pilgrimage*
*Randy and the Mob*

*American Beauty*
*Bernie*
*Biloxi Blues* ✤
*Brubaker*
*Chrystal*
*Guilty by Suspicion*

*A Soldier's Story*  
*Take Shelter*  
*Tender Mercies*  
*Winterhawk*  

*Monster's Ball*  
*October Sky*  
*The Paper Chase*  
*What's Eating Gilbert Grape*  

## Dishonorable Mentions (Worst of the Worst)

*Chopper Chicks in Zombietown*  
*The Conqueror*  
*Lady in a Cage*  
*The Monster and the Stripper*  
*The White River Kid*  

*Bloody Mama*  
*The Conqueror*  
*I'm from Arkansas*  
*The Monster and the Stripper*  
Any *Gator* film  

## Historical Importance (Critics Agree)

*Broncho Billy and the Schoolmistress*  
*Creature from the Black Lagoon*  
*A Face in the Crowd*  
*42nd Street*  
*The Great Train Robbery*  
*The Glass Key*  
*Hallelujah*  
*Shane*  
*True Grit* (1964)  
*Uncle Tom's Cabin* (1927)

# Bibliography

In addition to the works cited below, we frequently cross-checked biographical data, shooting locations, and release dates by recourse to various online references. The Internet Movie Database (IMDb) and the Internet Broadway Database (IBDb), in particular, were often utilized.

## GENERAL REFERENCES

Bogle, Donald. *Toms, Coons, Mulattoes, Mammies, & Bucks: An Interpretive History of Blacks in American Films.* New York: Continuum, 1973.

Cripps, Thomas. *Slow Fade to Black: The Negro in American Film, 1900–1942.* New York: Oxford University Press, 1977.

Dooley, Roger. *From Scarface to Scarlett: American Films in the 1930s.* New York: Harcourt, Brace, Jovanovich, 1984.

Easter, Alvin. *Lash!: The Hundred Great Scenes of Men Being Whipped in the Movies.* N.p.: Xlibris, 2004.

Etulain, Richard W., and Glenda Riley, eds. *The Hollywood West.* Golden, Colo.: Fulcrum, 2001.

Everson, William K. *American Silent Film.* 1978. Reprint, New York: Da Capo, 1998.

Friedman, Ryan J. *Hollywood's African American Films: The Transition to Sound.* New Brunswick, N.J.: Rutgers University Press, 2011.

Lewis, Jon. *American Film: A History.* New York: Norton, 2008.

McCarthy, Todd, and Charles Flynn. *Kings of the Bs: Working within the Hollywood System.* New York: E. P. Dutton, 1975.

Palmer, R. Barton. *Hollywood's Dark Cinema: The American Film Noir.* New York: Twayne, 1994.

Simmon, Scott. *The Invention of the Western Film: A Cultural History of the Genre's First Half-Century.* Cambridge: Cambridge University Press, 2003.

Smith, Andrew Brodie. *Shooting Cowboys and Indians: Silent Western Films, American Culture, and the Birth of Hollywood.* Boulder: University Press of Colorado, 2003.

Strausbaugh, John. *Black Like You: Blackface, Whiteface, Insult, & Imitation in American Popular Culture.* New York: Tarcher/Penguin, 2006.

Studlar, Gaylyn. "A Gunsel Is Being Beaten: Gangster Masculinity and the Homoerotics of the Crime Film." In *Mob Culture: Hidden Histories of the American Gangster Film,* edited by Lee Grieveson, Esther Sonnet, and Peter Stanfield, 120–45. New Brunswick, N.J.: Rutgers University Press, 2005.

Telotte, J. P. *Voices in the Dark: The Narrative Patterns of Film Noir.* Urbana: University of Illinois Press, 1989.

Tuska, Jon. *The Filming of the American West.* Garden City, N.Y.: Doubleday, 1976.

## SPECIFIC FILMS, DIRECTORS, and PERFORMERS

Beifuss, John. "From Locust Bayou It Came: Phil Chambliss, the Auteur from Arkansas." *Memphis Commercial Appeal,* August 30, 2007. http://blogs. commercialappeal.com/the_bloodshot_eye/2007/08/from-locust-bayou-it-came-phil-chambliss-the-auteur-from-arkansas.html.

Bledsoe, C. L. "Frank Bonner (1942–)." Last modified May 7, 2014. *Encyclopedia of Arkansas History and Culture.* http://www.encyclopedia ofarkansas.net/encyclopedia/entry-detail.aspx?entryID=3120.

———. "James Clarence (Jimmy) Wakely (1914–1982)." Last modified September 23, 2013. *Encyclopedia of Arkansas History and Culture.* http://www.encyclopediaofarkansas.net/encyclopedia/entry-detail. aspx?entryID=2787.

———. "Melinda Rose Dillon (1939–)." Last modified November 17, 2010. *Encyclopedia of Arkansas History and Culture.* http://www.encyclopedia ofarkansas.net/encyclopedia/entry-detail.aspx?entryID=3125.

Blevins, Brooks. *Arkansas/Arkansaw: How Bear Hunters, Hillbillies, & Good Ol' Boys Defined a State.* Fayetteville: University of Arkansas Press, 2009.

Browne, Turner. *The Last River: Life along Arkansas's Lower White.* Fayetteville: University of Arkansas Press, 1993.

Chilton, John. *Let the Good Times Roll: The Story of Louis Jordan and His Music.* Ann Arbor: University of Michigan Press, 1994.

Dickinson, Jim. "The Search for Blind Lemon." *Oxford American* 83 (2013): 104–24.

Dougan, Michael B. "William Caesar Warfield (1920–2002)." Last modified September 23, 2013. *Encyclopedia of Arkansas History and Culture.* http://www.encyclopediaofarkansas.net/encyclopedia/entry-detail.aspx?search=1&entryID=2789.

Durgnat, Raymond, and Scott Simmon. *King Vidor, American.* Berkeley: University of California Press, 1988.

Ebert, Roger. "*The Man in the Moon* (1991)." October 4, 1991. http://www.rogerebert.com/reviews/the-man-in-the-moon-1991.

Elrod, Denny. "Bob Burns (1890–1956)." Last modified July 25, 2013. *Encyclopedia of Arkansas History and Culture.* http://www.encyclopediaofarkansas.net/encyclopedia/entry-detail.aspx?search=1&entryID=2185.

Emberton, Jan. "Mary Nell Steenburgen (1953–)." Last modified June 4, 2014. *Encyclopedia of Arkansas History and Culture.* http://www.encyclopediaofarkansas.net/encyclopedia/entry-detail.aspx?entryID=29.

Enyeart, James L. *Willard Van Dyke: Changing the World through Photography and Film.* Albuquerque: University of New Mexico Press, 2008.

Erish, Andrew A. *Col. William N. Selig: The Man Who Invented Hollywood.* Austin: University of Texas Press, 2012.

Ford, Kody. "Home Grown: Kim Swink Brings Her Dream Film to the Screen." *The Idle Class* (blog), January 2, 2014. http://idleclassmag.com/valleyinnhomegrown/.

Frank, Amélie. "Billy Bob Thornton (1955–)." Last modified April 21, 2014. *Encyclopedia of Arkansas History and Culture.* http://www.encyclopediaofarkansas.net/encyclopedia/entry-detail.aspx?entryID=2174.

Gerstäcker, Friedrich. *Wild Sports: Rambling and Hunting Trips through the United States of North America.* Mechanicsburg, Pa.: Stackpole, 2004.

Gibron, Bill. "Boggy Down: Charles B. Pierce (1938–2010)." March 17, 2010. *Pop Matters.* http://www.popmatters.com/post/122119-boggy-down-charles-b.-pierce-1938-2010/.

Golden, Eve. *Vernon and Irene Castle's Ragtime Revolution.* Lexington: University Press of Kentucky, 2007.

Hall, Brenda J. "Freeman Harrison Owens (1890–1979)." Last modified March 25, 2013. *Encyclopedia of Arkansas History and Culture.* http://www.encyclopediaofarkansas.net/encyclopedia/entry-detail. aspx?entryID=66.

Hancock, Elliott. "Lloyd Andrews (1906–1992)." Last modified May 5, 2010. *Encyclopedia of Arkansas History and Culture.* http://www.encyclopedia ofarkansas.net/encyclopedia/entry-detail.aspx?entryID=4334.

Harris, Will. "Tess Harper on *Breaking Bad, Tender Mercies,* and Shooting Kevin Bacon." December 12, 2012. TV Club. *A.V. Club.* http://www. avclub.com/article/tess-harper-on-ibreaking-badi-itender-merciesi- and-89779.

Hartman, Lacy. "Joey Lauren Adams (1968–)." Last modified May 7, 2014. *Encyclopedia of Arkansas History and Culture.* http://www.encyclopedia ofarkansas.net/encyclopedia/entry-detail.aspx?entryID=4375.

Harvey, Dennis. "Phil Chambliss, Arkansas Auteur." November 15, 2007. *SF360.* http://www.sf360.org/?pageid=10394.

Helm, Levon, with Stephen Davis. *This Wheel's on Fire: Levon Helm and the Story of the Band.* New York: William Morrow, 1993.

Hendricks, Nancy. "Alan Ladd (1913–1964)." Last modified May 8, 2012. *Encyclopedia of Arkansas History and Culture.* http://www.encyclopedia ofarkansas.net/encyclopedia/entry-detail.aspx?entryID=2767.

———. "Ben Daniel Piazza (1933–1991)." Last modified August 8, 2012. *Encyclopedia of Arkansas History and Culture.* http://www.encyclopedia ofarkansas.net/encyclopedia/entry-detail.aspx?entryID=355.

———. "Charles Pierce (1938–2010)." Last modified September 7, 2010. *Encyclopedia of Arkansas History and Culture.* http://www.encyclopedia ofarkansas.net/encyclopedia/entry-detail.aspx?entryID=4398.

———. "Dale Evans (1912–2001)." Last modified August 21, 2013. *Encyclopedia of Arkansas, History and Culture.* http://www.encyclopedia ofarkansas.net/encyclopedia/entry-detail.aspx?entryID=2334.

———. "Gail Davis (1925–1997)." Last modified May 22, 2014. *Encyclopedia of Arkansas History and Culture.* http://www.encyclopediaofarkansas.net/ encyclopedia/entry-detail.aspx?entryID=2745.

———. "Harry Z. Thomason (1940–)." Last modified November 11, 2013. *Encyclopedia of Arkansas History and Culture.* http://www.encyclopedia ofarkansas.net/encyclopedia/entry-detail.aspx?entryID=2759.

———. "James Bridges (1936–1993)." Last modified May 26, 2011. *Encyclopedia of Arkansas History and Culture.* http://www.encyclopedia ofarkansas.net/encyclopedia/entry-detail.aspx?entryID=2740.

Herrington, Chris. "'Arkansas Auteur' Phil Chambliss at the Brooks." August 30, 2007. *Memphis Flyer.* http://www.memphisflyer.com/ memphis/arkansas-auteur-phil-chambliss-at-the-brooks/Content ?oid=1139054.

Hoskyns, Barney. *Across the Great Divide: The Band and America.* New York: Hyperion, 1993.

Jewison, Norman. *This Terrible Business Has Been Good to Me.* New York: T. Dunne, 2005.

Kael, Pauline. *Taking It All In.* New York: Holt, Rinehart, and Winston, 1984.

Kazan, Elia. *Elia Kazan: A Life.* New York: Da Capa Press, 1997.

———. *Kazan on Directing.* New York: Vintage Books, 2009.

Kiehn, David. *Broncho Billy and the Essanay Film Company.* Berkeley, Calif.: Farwell, 2003.

King, Susan. "'True Grit' Memories from Kim Darby and Glen Campbell." January 4, 2011. *Los Angeles Times.* http://articles.latimes.com/2011/ jan/04/entertainment/la-et-true-grit-nostalgia-20110104.

Koch, Stephen. "Louis Thomas Jordan (1908–1975)." Last modified March 5, 2014. *Encyclopedia of Arkansas History and Culture.* http://www. encyclopediaofarkansas.net/encyclopedia/entry-detail.aspx?entry ID=1685.

Koon, David. "Harold Brett 'Hal' Needham (1931–)." Last modified May 22, 2014. *Encyclopedia of Arkansas History and Culture.* http://www. encyclopediaofarkansas.net/encyclopedia/entry-detail.aspx?entry ID=6944.

———. "Man on Fire: A Q&A with Writer/Director/Stuntman Hal Needham." June 1, 2011. *Arkansas Times.* http://www.arktimes.com/ arkansas/man-on-fire/Content?oid=1764548.

———. "The World's Most Interesting Man." June 1, 2011. *Arkansas Times.*

http://www.arktimes.com/arkansas/the-worlds-most-interesting man/
Content?oid=1764541.

Majors, Allison. "Jerry Van Dyke (1931–)." Last modified April 14, 2014.
*Encyclopedia of Arkansas History and Culture.* http://www.encyclopedia
ofarkansas.net/encyclopedia/entry-detail.aspx?search=1&entryID=4386.

Martin, Douglas. "Rudy Ray Moore, 81, a Precursor of Rap, Dies."
October 22, 2008. *New York Times.* http://www.nytimes.com/2008/
10/22/movies/22moore.html?_r=0.

Martin, Philip. "Review: *War Eagle, Arkansas.*" June 12, 2009. *Arkansas
Online.* http://www.arkansasonline.com/news/2009/jun/12/review-
war-eagle-arkansas-20090612/?entertainment/movies.

———. "Your Monkey's Take on *Bernie.*" *blood, dirt & angels* (blog),
May 30, 2012. http://www.blooddirtandangels.com/index.php/2012/
05/30/your-monkeys-take-on-bernie/.

McNeil, W. K. "Dick Powell (1904–1963)." Last modified August 19, 2009.
*Encyclopedia of Arkansas History and Culture.* http://www.encyclopedia
ofarkansas.net/encyclopedia/entry-detail.aspx?entryID=1741.

Melnick, Ross. *American Showman: Samuel "Roxy" Rothafel and the Birth of
the Entertainment Industry, 1908–1935.* New York: Columbia University
Press, 2012.

Mencken, H. L. "Famine." *Baltimore Evening Sun,* January 19, 1931, 17.

Messina, Cheryl. "Winona Sammon (1907–1941)." Last modified July 6, 2011.
*Encyclopedia of Arkansas History and Culture.* http://www.encyclopedia
ofarkansas.net/encyclopedia/entry-detail.aspx?entryID=3683.

Murton, Tom, and Joe Hyams. *Accomplices to the Crime.* New York: Grove,
1969.

Needham, Hal. *Stuntman!: My Car-Crashing, Plane-Jumping, Bone-Breaking,
Death-Defying Hollywood Life.* New York: Little, Brown, 2011.

Pendarvis, Jack. "From Hoofer to Gumshoe: Tailing Sly Dick Powell."
*Oxford American* 56 (2007): 34–39.

Pierce, David. "'Carl Laemmle's Outstanding Achievement': Harry Pollard
and the Struggle to Film *Uncle Tom's Cabin.*" *Film History* 10 (1998):
459–76.

Portis, Charles. *True Grit.* New York: Simon and Schuster, 1968.

Reynolds, David S. *Mightier Than the Sword:* Uncle Tom's Cabin *and the Battle for America*. New York: W. W. Norton, 2011.

Ricks, Brandi. "An Interview with Arkansas Filmmaker Juli Jackson." December 5, 2012. *Hexbeat*. http://hexbeat.com/an-interview-with-arkansas-filmmaker-juli-jackson/.

Schuette, Shirley Sticht. "*Die Goldsucher von Arkansas* [Movie]." Last modified March 5, 2012. *Encyclopedia of Arkansas History and Culture*. http://www.encyclopediaofarkansas.net/encyclopedia/entry-detail.aspx?entryID=4844.

Schulberg, Budd. *Some Faces in the Crowd*. Chicago: Ivan R. Dee, 2008.

Slide, Anthony. *The Encyclopedia of Vaudeville*. Westport, Conn.: Greenwood, 1994.

Sobel, Ken. *Babe Ruth & the American Dream*. New York: Ballantine Books, 1974.

Stephens, Chuck. "A Face in the Crowd: Jay C. Flippen." March 11, 2013. *Film Comment*. http://www.filmcomment.com/article/a-face-in-the-crowd-jay-c.-flippen.

Stewart, Shea. "*Slow Southern Steel* Captivates with True Stories." January 24, 2012. *Sync*. http://www.syncweekly.com/news/2012/jan/24/slow-southern-steel-captivates-true-stories/.

Stouffer, Marty. *Marty Stouffer's Wild America*. New York: Times Books, 1988.

Takei, George. *To the Stars*. New York: Pocket Books, 1994.

Teske, Anastasia. "Irene Castle (1893–1969)." Last modified June 16, 2010. *Encyclopedia of Arkansas History and Culture*. http://www.encyclopediaofarkansas.net/encyclopedia/entry-detail.aspx?entryID=5649.

Tonguette, Peter. *The Films of James Bridges*. Jefferson, N.C.: McFarland, 2011.

Vidor, King. *King Vidor on Film Making*. New York: David McKay, 1972.

Wallace, Michele. "*Uncle Tom's Cabin b*efore and after the Jim Crow Era." *Drama Review* 44, no. 1 (2000): 137–56.

Wallis, Dave. "'Broncho Billy' Anderson (1880–1971)." Last modified April 14, 2008. *Encyclopedia of Arkansas History and Culture*. http://www.encyclopediaofarkansas.net/encyclopedia/entry-detail.aspx?entryID=534.

Ware, Hames. "Arthur Lee Hunnicutt (1910–1979)." Last modified May 5, 2010. *Encyclopedia of Arkansas History and Culture.* http://www.encyclopediaofarkansas.net/encyclopedia/entry-detail. aspx?entryID=3178.

Warfield, William, and Alton Miller. *My Music & My Life.* Champaign, Ill.: Sagamore, 1991.

White, Raymond E. *King of the Cowboys, Queen of the West: Roy Rogers and Dale Evans.* Madison: University of Wisconsin Press, 2005.

Wolfe, Ron. "Still the Gill Man's Gal." *Arkansas Democrat-Gazette,* May 7, 2013.

Young, Jeff. *Kazan: The Master Director Discusses His Films; Interviews with Elia Kazan.* New York: New Market Press, 1999.

# Index